NO MAGIC HELICOPTER

An Aging Amazon's Climb of Mount Everest

Carol Masheter,
also known as the SilverFox

Aventine Press

Published by Aventine Press
750 State St. #319
San Diego CA, 92101
www.aventinepress.com

ISBN: 1-59330-698-9

Library of Congress Control Number: 2010918502
Library of Congress Cataloging-in-Publication Data
No Magic Helicopter

Printed in the United States of America

This book is dedicated to all those who face challenges,
both welcome and unwelcome.

Acknowledgements

I am grateful for encouragement and generosity from many people. Without their help my climb of Everest or this book would not have been possible.

I thank my sister, Linda, for her patience with my crazy adventures. Long climbs on big mountains can be hard on those we love. Linda, I appreciate your tolerance. I also thank my late parents, my first and best teachers. They set high standards and expected me to meet them, for which I am grateful.

At the Utah Department of Health, where I work, David Sundwall, M.D., Keely Cofrin Allen, Ph.D., and Wu Xu, Ph.D., believed in my dream to climb Everest as much as I did. My other colleagues graciously continued our work during my absence. I appreciate their generous support.

Professional mountaineering guides, Javier Herrera and Ben Marshall, encouraged me to try Everest. Brian Cox, Mark Johnson, Mike Hamill, Calvin Hebert, and Alasdair Turner, helped me gain the necessary high-altitude experience and the skills. Thanks, guys.

I could not have climbed Everest without the guidance and support of our guides, climbing Sherpas, and Base Camp staff. The director of Adventure Consultants, Guy Cotter; the expedition leader, Mike Roberts; and guides, Lydia Bradey, Victor Saunders, and

Ang Dorje Sherpa, were willing to take a chance on me, an amateur woman mountaineer in her 60s. Base Camp Sirdar (Sherpa leader), Ang Tsering Sherpa; Head Chef, Chhongba Sherpa; and Base Camp Managers, Laurel Morrison and Suze Kelly, transformed a stark maze of rock and ice into a home away from home.

The Adventure Consultants Sherpas have my undying respect and appreciation. They have a quiet strength, patience, and humility I try to emulate and often fail to attain. Thank you, Tendi Bai (younger brother) and Nima Bai, for doing your best to keep me safe under difficult circumstances. Many others quietly and capably provided invaluable support. They include Lhakpa Dorje Sherpa, Phu Tashi Sherpa, Dawa Zangbu Sherpa, Sangay Dorje Sherpa, Ang Sona Sherpa, Temba Sherpa, Pemba Choti Sherpa, Namgyal Sherpa, Passang Bhote #1 and Passang Bhote #2, and Zangbu Sherpa as well as our Base Camp Sherpa staff, Camp 2 staff, yak men, and porters. Namaste and thank you.

Several people started me on this path, though perhaps they, like me, never imagined it would include climbing Everest. Steve Coulter, Walt Haas, Steve Walker, and Kyle Williams, taught me basic mountaineering skills in the Wasatch Mountains near Salt Lake, Utah. Bill Thompson gave me solid advice about gaining the necessary skills and high altitude mountaineering experience. Scott Carson and his colleagues at International Mountain Equipment (IME) in Salt Lake have encouraged me, a woman who started climbing late in life, for nearly two decades.

Dozens of friends from work, my yoga community, the Wasatch Mountain Club, and my meditation sangha (community) followed Internet dispatches and emails about my adventure. No doubt their prayers and good thoughts helped keep me safe.

Several friends gave me a hero's farewell, even after my climb seemed over before it began. Their enthusiasm and optimism helped me overcome discouragement as my dream appeared to be unraveling. I will never forget that farewell dinner or their over-the-top welcome home.

Several people encouraged me to write this book. Thank you, Cyndi Bemis, Douglas M. Brown, Jamie Martell, and Mike Martin, for your encouragement and feedback. Thank you, Mark Gaskill and Bruce Tremper, for suggestions about publishing.

Contents

"Avoiding danger is no safer than outright exposure.
Life is a daring adventure or nothing at all." Helen Keller

Why Do Climbers Climb?

June 3, 2009. Bad weather had trapped us midway up the mountain for 11 days. Then a welcome break came between storms, and we had eagerly climbed the rugged ridge of rock, snow, and ice up to the highest camp. We needed one more good day to climb the last 3,000 vertical feet to the summit. Another storm of driving snow and high winds rolled in with a vengeance. Time had run out. It was time to descend and start a chain of plane flights home. Feeling sick with disappointment, I huddled in my tent and stuffed my down sleeping bag into its compression sack.

Tears filled my eyes and splashed onto my gloves, as I packed my gear. I felt silly about crying over a mountain, but hauling enough food, fuel, and equipment up the highest peak in North America had been very hard. If I wanted to summit Denali, I would need to return next year, after another season of hard training. I was not sure I had it in me. Then I remembered crying about another mountain for very different reasons. That mountain was Everest.

This is my story about the climb of my life. It describes what led me to try Mount Everest as an amateur woman mountaineer in my 60s, how I prepared, and what the climb was like for me. My account is subject to possible distortions of memory due to demands the climb made on me physically and emotionally. Others who were on Everest in the spring of 2008 may remember events differently.

Some climbers have written eloquently about their own Everest experience, the history of climbing Everest, the beauty of the Khumbu region where Everest is located, and the remarkable Sherpa people, without whose strength and skill most Westerners would have little chance of summiting the world's highest mountain. I strongly recommend that readers read their books as well as mine.

I was an unlikely Everest climber. A woman in her early 60s, I was not very impressive looking -- five feet six inches tall and weighing about 135 lbs. I took medication for anxiety, depression, irritable bowel, and hypothyroidism. I was afraid of heights. Why would someone like me even consider climbing Everest, the highest mountain in the world?

There are probably as many reasons to climb Everest as there are climbers. My own climb was neither a lifelong dream nor a whim. My climb evolved from a life-long drive to do something outstanding and my fascination with big mountains. Perhaps I wanted to leave some record of my time on earth. Perhaps, as one Nobel Prize laureate put it, I was looking for love.

My earliest memory of wanting to do something outstanding was a childhood daydream while in the hospital. In the summer of 1953, when I was almost 7, my mother, younger sister, Linda, and I flew from our home in Southern California to Kansas for my grandfather's funeral. My father stayed home, as he had limited vacation time from his job as an engineer. While we were in Kansas, my sister and I became ill. A local doctor in the small farm town of Pratt, near the even tinier town of Isabel where my grandmother lived, suspected we had polio and sent us on a tense midnight drive to Wichita for a formal diagnosis. There, I was terrified of the huge syringe used to perform the spinal tap. I fought like a wild cat, while a burly nurse tried to hold me still.

When the spinal tap confirmed that we both had polio, Linda and I were immediately sent to a polio isolation ward. It was hot and humid. The hospital had no air conditioning. We wore only cotton underpants and lay sweating on top of our sheets. The treatment for polio of the time seemed like torture. The intravenous horse serum made me vomit, until I was delirious. The steaming hot blankets blistered my skin, when nurses wrapped them around my naked arms, legs, and torso. Between torture sessions, nurses told me I was not allowed to sit up or get out of bed, or I would be paralyzed for life. Lying flat on my back 24/7, I daydreamed of doing something heroic when I got out of the hospital, like rescuing a drowning swimmer by the time I was 8 years old. Remembering my terrified thrashing in the deep end of the local pool earlier that summer, I made plans to become a better swimmer.

Finally doctors allowed me to leave my bed for the first time in weeks. Wearing heavy corrective shoes, I shuffled clumsily a few feet from my hospital bed and toppled into the arms of a nurse. I was weak, the arches in my feet were flat, and my back swayed alarmingly, but I could walk. I had escaped paralysis, as had my sister. At the time, I did not realize how fortunate I was. I was just really glad to get out of that cursed bed.

Back at home in Southern California, I did physical therapy every evening in the living room under my parents' supervision. I picked up marbles with my toes, until my feet cramped. I squeezed a nickel between my buttocks, until my back ached. I did sit ups, until I could do no more. I had to wear heavy leather corrective shoes, while my friends wore sneakers and seemed to run like the wind.

My parents were afraid I would injure my weakened back, so they forbad me to lift the garage door to get my bike. When no one was looking, I would sneak outside and lift the heavy door like a giant barbell as many times as I could before grabbing my bike and peddling around the neighborhood. When my parents caught me, their disapproval hurt and their spankings stung, but I was determined not to be weak. If there were any silver linings to having polio, they were this early determination to be strong and the dream of doing something extraordinary. Why I reacted this way and did not accept a role of being "weak" or "sick" is still a mystery to me.

Polio, daily exercises, and corrective shoes were not the only things that set me apart. In the 1950s and 1960s rich girls went to finishing school to learn how to carry a suitcase, so their muscles would not show. I was more interested in riding horses and finishing first in school foot races. I wanted muscles, and I wanted them to show. Though I was more active than most kids my age and earned good grades in school, I was terribly shy. I had acne starting at age 9 and was painfully self-conscious about it. Selling Girl Scout cookies door to door, leaving fliers on people's porches for my mother's real estate business, and even answering the family telephone were agony. As a teenager, when my father dropped me off at the Methodist church for dances, I hid all evening in the bushes outside the social hall to avoid being asked to dance.

While other kids my age were going nuts over Elvis Presley, I fell in love with classical music. As a young teen, I dreamed of becoming a concert pianist and traveling the world to perform pieces by Mozart, Vivaldi, and Chopin, a curious dream for someone as shy as I was. After the launch of Sputnik, my school advisors noticed my aptitude for science and encouraged me in that direction. I liked science as well as music. On weekends after my piano lesson, I would ride my bike three miles to the local library and read "Scientific American." I dreamed of making great scientific discoveries. I had no shortage of grand ideas, but I was not very talented in either music or science. My earnest diligence made me just good enough to fuel my ambitious dreams.

On some Saturdays, two other unconventional girls and I persuaded one of our parents to get up early and drive us to the Irvine Ranch, which in the early 1960s was still undeveloped land. We would spend the entire day hiking through hills of tall sun-cured grass and live oak, dodging herds of range cattle and avoiding clumps of prickly pear cactus, while keeping our eyes open for rattle snakes. I loved hiking up to a view point and gazing over the rolling hills. I felt confident and strong, away from the traffic, noise, and smog of where I lived, away from mean-spirited classmates who teased me about my acne.

Mary Tamara Utens, one of my hiking friends, showed me her older brother's Eddie Bauer catalogs. In the 1960's Eddie Bauer specialized in expedition down sleeping bags and clothing. I marveled at the pictures of mountaineers standing on snowy summits wearing puffy parkas, mountaineering boots, and crampons (metal spikes that mountaineers strap onto the soles of their boots to grip ice and hard snow). Climbing big mountains seemed really cool but completely out of reach for me. Surely only world-class mountaineers climbed such mountains, not awkward pimply teenage girls like me.

A Phoenix From Ashes

The busy-ness of life pushed the Eddie Bauer pictures of mountains to the back of my mind for awhile. Becoming a scientist seemed like a more realistic career plan than becoming a concert pianist. In 1968 I graduated from UCLA in chemistry and accepted a job as a research chemist at Wesleyan University in Middletown, Connecticut. I had never been further east than Arkansas, and though still painfully shy, I was eager to explore life as a newly launched adult. With my first paychecks I bought a Kelty external frame backpack and a down sleeping bag. At the apartment I shared with two other young women, I tested the sleeping bag in my unheated attic bedroom. After shivering inside the bag for the first 15 minutes to warm it up, it never failed me, even when temperatures dipped below zero degrees Fahrenheit. Emboldened, I did several backpack trips with the Sierra Club. I loved backpacking in wilderness and climbing peaks in the Sierras and the Rockies. As much as I enjoyed living in central Connecticut with its pretty patchwork of fields, forests, towns, and cities, I lived for those annual backpack trips in the rugged mountains of the West.

I tried climbing even higher mountains. In 1972, I went to East Africa and climbed high on Mt. Kenya. Unlike the triumphant joy I had felt on previous summits in the Rockies and Sierras, on

Point Lenana at 16,355 feet elevation, I experienced tunnel vision, lassitude, and a terrible headache. Later I learned these are the classic symptoms of moderate altitude sickness, probably exacerbated by dehydration due to a nasty case of travelers' diarrhea. Happily, I was able to descend from Point Lenana under my own power. A week later I climbed 3,000 feet higher to the crater rim of Mt. Kilimanjaro by the Marangu Route. Though I did not experience symptoms as intense as those on Point Lenana, I still felt dull, sick, and tired. I was glad to have tried both mountains, but the climbs were cold and joyless.

Hiking up big mountains was only one of my youthful explorations. I pushed myself to overcome my shyness and dated. I fell in love with a guy who did not feel the same way about me. I learned to scuba dive, so I could dive with my next boyfriend. He also was less involved with me than I was with him, a pattern that I would repeat several times with other men. Perhaps I felt more in control as the pursuer than the pursued. Between failed relationships, I drove my VW beetle up the then unpaved Alcan Highway and explored parts of Alaska. I raised and trained Morgan horses. I trained for and ran the Boston Marathon as a qualified runner. Some of these experiences were fun and rewarding. Others were painful. They all helped me figure out who I was and what I wanted out of life.

After a dozen years of working at universities as a research chemist, I decided to change careers. Though I loved research, I was not setting the world on fire as a scientist and wanted to get into something more people related. My childhood fantasy of saving a drowning swimmer had evolved into wanting to be some kind of healer or teacher. I wanted to help people more directly than working in a lab. In the 1980s I earned a masters degree in marriage and family therapy then a doctorate from the University of Connecticut in Storrs. In 1988 I accepted a tenure track position at Rutgers University in New Brunswick, New Jersey. The department that hired me was forced to merge with another department and expected me to publish in nutritional sciences instead of the area of my graduate work. I knew I needed to find a better professional fit.

Two years later I accepted another tenure track position at the University of Utah in Salt Lake. I settled into the life of an assistant professor, teaching classes, doing research, and applying for research grants. I had moved to Salt Lake to work, but I soon discovered the nearby mountains. I joined the Wasatch Mountain Club, a local outdoor club, and hiked with other members on the weekends. I met a guy who liked nerdy outdoorsy women like me. He taught me to rock climb and backcountry ski. We enjoyed talking about science and seemed to "get" each other. We became a couple.

My career bloomed. I published sole-author papers in the top peer-review publications in my field. Several times I was a finalist for my college's superior teaching award. I seemed to be on my way to doing something extraordinary, building a legacy as an innovative researcher and a respected teacher. At last, in my 40s, I seemed to have found my life's work and my life partner. Better late than never.

In 1995 a university colleague and fellow Wasatch Mountain Club member, Bill Thompson, summited Cho Oyu, whose name means Turquoise Goddess in Tibetan. The sixth highest peak in the world, Cho Oyu is in the Himalayas near Everest on the border between Tibet and Nepal. The Eddie Bauer pictures of climbers on big mountains resurfaced in my fantasies and rekindled my imagination. I thought real people like Bill can do this! Maybe I can too.

I took Bill to dinner and asked him how to prepare for such a climb. Bill's advice was clear and to the point. "No reputable company will guide you up a peak like Cho Oyu without experience at high altitude and the right set of skills. Build a mountaineering resume. Climb with a respected guide service, like American Alpine Institute [a climbing school and mountain guide company based in Bellingham, Washington.] You can get a lot climbing experience in South America." I thought perhaps after I had tenure, I could go to South America for a three week vacation and climb.

Starting in 1997, I experienced several major losses within 18 months. I lost a hard struggle for tenure. My department claimed

I was not publishing enough. When I had asked how many publications would be enough, they would not tell me. Then I learned my boyfriend of six years was involved with someone else. Hurt and angry, I ended our relationship. My sister became seriously ill in Albuquerque, New Mexico, where she lived. My mother died suddenly in Southern California. I felt devastated – again and again. I felt as though I was being attacked by wild beasts, ripped open, and left to bleed to death.

I did not know who I was or where I was going. A failed professor at age 50, I became a student again. I took university courses in computer science, calculus, and physics, sometimes along side my former students. "What are you doing here, Dr. Masheter?" some asked. "Learning something new, like you," I would shrug and reply. I avoided the topic of being denied tenure, because talking about it brought back an overwhelming sense of anger and shame. I worked several low-paying part-time jobs as a computer instructor and programmer to reduce the drain on my savings. Perhaps I needed to prove I was a smart worthwhile person. Perhaps I was punishing myself for failing as a professor and as a relationship partner, for not seeing my elderly mother and my only sister more often.

Stress piled up from grief, anger, overwork, and anxiety about my professional and financial future. Some nights I awoke screaming in pain, my legs locked rigid by muscle cramps. My innards felt as though invisible hands were twisting my intestines into those silly balloon figures for kids. I lost 15 lbs. and felt weak and tired.

The weight loss concerned me enough to see a doctor. He reassured me that I did not have cancer, an ulcer, or some other horrible disease. He referred me to a nutritionist and a gastrointestinal specialist. Both concluded I had severe irritable bowel syndrome. The nutritionist recommended smaller more frequent meals, eating yogurt with live cultures, and avoiding wheat. The GI specialist recommended I eat more wheat bran, contradicting the nutritionist's advice. Go figure, I grumbled to myself.

I experimented with the specialists' contradictory suggestions. Those that made me feel worse I stopped. Those that eased painful symptoms I continued. The leg cramps turned out to be symptoms of hypothyroidism. The cramps became less frequent and less severe, after I started taking thyroid medication. Estrogen and progesterone were prescribed to reduce my hot flashes and help me sleep better. They did not improve my sleep and made my intestinal symptoms worse, so I quit taking them. Gradually I began to feel better.

Slowly, some things became clear. I wanted to stay in Salt Lake. It felt like home. Hiking, climbing, and backcountry skiing with friends in the nearby Wasatch Mountains was a big part of my life. Perhaps now would be a good time to try climbing in the Andes. Taking a foreign trip when my financial future was so unsettled seemed counter intuitive. However, I saw this trip as a "vacation" from the anger, sadness, and stress I was experiencing. Instead of the happy celebration I had imagined after getting tenure, my start in high-altitude mountaineering was born from loss and pain. I rose like a phoenix rising from ashes.

Turquoise Goddess

At 50 years of age, I signed up for climbing instruction and mountaineering in the Bolivian Andes with the American Alpine Institute. There I became the student of Brian Cox, a guide half my age. Brian did an excellent job of teaching mountaineering skills. He instructed four guys and me in crampon techniques, how to climb as members of a rope team, safe route finding on glaciers, ice climbing with two ice tools, and mixed climbing on rock, snow, and ice. Brian stressed the importance of adequate hydration and caloric intake, gradual acclimatization, and pacing. He was patient and positive.

Brian's instruction contrasted sharply with my experience on Mt. Kenya and Mt. Kilimanjaro. Since the early 70s, knowledge about reducing the risk of altitude sickness had improved. Thanks to Brian's gradual acclimatization program and insistence that we drink plenty of water, I had no problems with altitude sickness in Bolivia and climbed four peaks ranging in elevation from 17,000 to 21,000 feet.

Climbing in the Andes pushed my abilities and taught me a lot. Of course, I doubted my sanity during the miserable moments, like when four of us climbed to 21,000 feet elevation in a driving snow storm. However, the moments of doubt and misery paled compared to the joy of summiting high, icy peaks with melodious names like

Eslovania, Piramide Blanca, Ilusion, and Illimani. I had such a wonderful time, I returned to climb in South America and summited additional peaks: Piqueno Alpamayo, Huayna Potosi, Janko Uyu, Culim Thojo, Illiniza Norte, Cayambe, Cotopaxi, and Chimborazo. Climbing to the top of big mountains on my first attempt began to feel routine, the logical outcome of getting very fit, buying the right gear, learning appropriate skills, drinking only treated water, eating only properly prepared food, and taking enough time to acclimatize properly.

I had so much fun climbing in South America, the dream of climbing Cho Oyu faded for awhile. However as I approached my 60th birthday, several guides encouraged me to try the Turquoise Goddess. I was strong and fit for a woman of my age, but each year I lost a little speed and power. I got injured more easily and took longer to recover. Somewhere I read inactive people lose 3% of their strength every year, while active people lose only 0.5% a year. Apparently we can slow the aging process, but we cannot stop it.

If I wanted to try Cho Oyu, I needed to do it soon, or I would be too weak. I had recently started a new career in public health, and my vacation time was very limited. I would need permission to take an unpaid leave of six weeks from my new job with the Utah Department of Health to climb Cho Oyu.

In the spring of 2005, I dropped hints. My boss, Wu Xu, was a bright volatile Chinese woman, who came of age during the Cultural Revolution. Not allowed to go to high school, she and her friends read banned books and secretly educated themselves at considerable risk. I admired her fierce determination to learn. I hoped she could relate to my climb of Cho Oyu. When I asked her for permission to take unpaid leave, Wu exploded, "Why you want do that?! Too dangerous! You die up there!" Her reaction surprised me. For a moment, I froze, not knowing how to respond. Then I heard myself say quietly, "Wu, people die right here in car wrecks every day." Wu walked away, shaking her head in disbelief that I wanted to do such a crazy thing.

Now what? I wondered. Do I quit my job to climb a mountain? My chances of finding another job I liked as well as this one at nearly 60 years of age did not seem good. Climbing big mountains in distant countries was an expensive hobby. I could not afford to retire and climb fulltime. The next morning I was settling into my work, when Wu approached me tentatively. "If climbing this mountain is your dream, I support you anyway I can," she said quietly. The change was so unexpected, I was numb with surprise. "OK," I grinned. I walked on air for days.

My next step was choosing an expedition. I was going to climb a mountain nearly 27,000 feet in elevation on the other side of the world. I wanted to optimize my chances for a safe summit and return. I wanted the best leadership and resources I could afford. American Alpine Institute, the company with which I had had so many enjoyable climbs in South America, was affiliated with Adventure Consultants. Based in New Zealand, Adventure Consultants runs deeply resourced expeditions with top-notch guides. They are expensive, but they have had a good safety record for guiding amateur climbers up some of the world's highest peaks, including Cho Oyu and Everest.

With some trepidation I sent my application and climbing resume to Adventure Consultants. At the time the oldest client they had guided on Cho Oyu was 53 years of age. I was nearly 59. To my surprise and delight, they accepted me. After I had met and talked with a younger Salt Lake man who had summited Cho Oyu without supplemental oxygen, I wanted to "climb pure" like him. Because I seemed to have solved my altitude problems in the Andes, I expected no problems climbing almost 6,000 vertical feet higher to the summit of Cho Oyu. I trained hard. By the departure date in late August, I felt ready and confident.

My Cho Oyu experience could fill another book. However, this book is about Everest, so it includes only the highlights of lessons learned on other mountains. Climbing in the Andes made me confident, even cocky. Cho Oyu cut me down to size. At Advanced Base Camp at 18,300 feet elevation, I slept poorly and felt lousy much of the time. Eating higher on the mountain was nearly impossible, a problem I had not experienced previously. I went from being the strongest climber on some of my South American climbs to the weakest of our team to summit Cho Oyu. When I staggered the last few steps to the top, I was so happy I wanted to jump over the moon, but all I could do was kneel in the snow and gasp for air. My usual triumphant summit howl, "aaahhhooo… (cough, hack, cough, cough)," sounded like a dying animal. I stared dully at the summit of Everest, another 2,100 vertical feet higher and about 13 miles east as the crow flies. My team mates chattered excitedly about trying Everest next. That day I could not imagine climbing a single foot higher.

Cho Oyu is a popular practice peak for climbers who want to try Everest. After I returned home, friends asked me whether I wanted to climb Everest. I said no and meant it. Each step to the summit of Cho Oyu had been a sheer act of will.

I could think of many reasons not to climb Everest besides my own physical limitations. I had read that Everest attracted too many people with big egos, too much money, and not enough high altitude mountaineering experience. It also attracted people trying to climb "on the cheap." With few resources they had little chance of summiting and were at high risk of getting into serious trouble and putting others at increased risk. Accounts of the deaths and injuries in Jon Krakauer's "Into Thin Air" terrified me. Everest seemed too crowded, too risky, too expensive, and beyond my abilities. I was so happy to have summited Cho Oyu. I considered it to be my "swan song" for climbing big mountains. I sold my new down suit and down sleeping bag, rated to minus 40 degrees, on eBay, figuring I would not need them again.

The following year, I learned that Ana Boscarioli, my tent mate on Cho Oyu, summited Everest, becoming the first Brazilian woman to do so. Thoughts about big crowds, high price tags, death, and injury evaporated. If she can do it, maybe I can too, chirped my inner optimist. Then my voice of reason argued, Ana is 20 years younger than you. On most days above 20,000 feet elevation she was stronger than you. Get real.

Even with these doubts, I could not stop thinking about Everest. Some experts claim the body remembers altitude. Perhaps if I climbed high again, my body would adapt better. Maybe I could find foods I could eat and keep down. Maybe I could find ways to sleep better. If I could solve these problems, I would have a reasonable chance on Everest.

The Right Stuff

The idea of climbing Aconcagua intrigued me. At 22,840 feet elevation, it is the highest peak in the Western Hemisphere. It could be a good test to see whether my body could adapt better to high altitude after summiting Cho Oyu. Aconcagua in Argentina was closer and cheaper than trying another big peak in the Himalayas.

Though I summited Aconcagua in January, 2007, my body did not remember attitude. Above 19,000 feet elevation, I had not been able to sleep or eat better than on Cho Oyu. I was slower than my younger male guides and team members. I was happy about summiting, but with no solutions to my problems with eating, sleeping, and shortness of breath at high altitude, my Everest prospects did not look promising.

A few months after Aconcagua, I learned that Chuck McGibbon, another of the four of us who summited Cho Oyu together, had climbed to the South Summit of Everest. There, Chuck had turned back due to exhaustion. The South Summit is about 300 vertical feet below and about a quarter mile from the actual summit. Turning back "so close" to the summit may puzzle people who have not been there. However, the last stretch, known as the Knife Edge, is a narrow jagged ridge of rock, ice, and snow above 28,500 feet elevation. Drop offs plunge down both sides for thousands of feet.

One misstep could have deadly consequences. The Knife Edge includes the famous Hillary Step, considered to be the most difficult part of the climb. When climbers get to the South Summit, they have been climbing for many hours, often in subzero temperatures, eating and drinking little. For a cold exhausted climber standing on the South Summit, the true summit might as well be on the moon.

Chuck was an amazing guy -- a retired calculus professor, Sudoku practitioner, and rock climber. Though he was a couple of years older than me, he was stronger than me on Cho Oyu. If he did not summit Everest, what chance would I have? Yet for some crazy reason, Chuck's climb to the South Summit made me want to try. I wanted to make it three out of the four of us who summited Cho Oyu together to try Everest. Chuck came so close. Maybe I could learn from his experience.

I hesitated to contact Chuck. I could only imagine how disappointed he must have been to have climbed so high without summiting. However, after a few weeks, I could not resist. He did not answer my email. I was disappointed but not surprised. Then months later I received a reply from him. He had been abroad and had not accessed his usual email account for awhile.

Chuck's advice was concise. "Don't skimp on your boots, down clothing, or sleeping bag." Chuck had trouble keeping warm high on Everest. "Don't get sick." Chuck had come down with a nasty GI bug just before his final climb, which weakened him. "Don't give the guides any reason to turn you back before the summit." This last suggestion puzzled me. I could not imagine Chuck giving anyone any reason to turn him back, because he had been so strong on Cho Oyu.

I considered Chuck's advice carefully. If I decided to try Everest, I would make sure I had the best boots, down parka, and down sleeping bag. I could take precautions to lower the risk of getting sick. I interpreted Chuck's last piece of advice to mean I should get in the best shape of my life.

Climbing Everest is a huge commitment. The time needed to acclimatize and climb the mountain takes about two months. Also, climbers are more likely to reach the summit and return safely, if they have learned the required mountaineering skills and gained high altitude experience, physical fitness, and mental toughness before attempting Everest.

As numerous books and documentaries have made clear, climbing Everest is dangerous. I asked myself again and again, can I accept the risk of permanent injury or even dying on the mountain? Can I face the displeasure of a worried sister and concerned friends? Can I take two months of unpaid leave from work and still keep my job? Can I get strong enough to climb over 2,000 feet higher than the summit of Cho Oyu? If I tried and failed to summit Everest, could I live with that? Did I have the "right stuff?"

I was not sure.

I spent several months reading books and watching documentaries on Everest, trying to assess whether I had what it takes. The Discovery Channel's "Everest: Beyond the Limit, Season 1" was especially helpful. It highlighted hazards from traffic jams that expose even well-prepared climbers to additional hours of extreme cold and low oxygen, putting them at increased risk for injury or death. It described the difficulties of rescue high on the mountain, especially of climbers who can not move on their own. Capable rescuers are not often available at the right time and the right place above 26,000 feet elevation.

The documentary's treatment of "summit fever" made an especially strong impression on me. To summit, climbers need a fierce determination to push through fatigue and cold for many hours. However, such determination can drive people to complete exhaustion, and then they collapse and die. I have that kind determination. I have pushed myself through pain and hypothermia to complete other ambitious climbs, marathons, a 76-mile rugged wilderness hike in 26 hours, and a 200-mile bike ride in one day. If I injured myself or died on Everest, I could "live" with that. However, I did not feel right about putting others at unnecessary risk, especially Sherpas.

Climbing Sherpas are rock stars, admired in their own culture as well as ours. They climb above Base Camp, establish higher camps, carry loads of supplies, and accompany client climbers and guides to the summit. Like us, they can become seriously ill from altitude sickness. A disproportionate number of Sherpas have died on Everest. If Sherpas had other career options that paid as well, many would not climb. Some say they climb so their sons do not have to. Some Sherpanis (women Sherpas) do not want to marry climbing Sherpas, because they do not want to become widows.

To lessen the chance that I might put others at risk, I made an appointment for a thorough medical exam. If the exam uncovered something that could "blow up" and become a problem on the mountain, I would not try Everest. During my annual check up, I asked my internist to perform an EKG. Based on some minor abnormalities in my scan, she ordered a stress test. The results confirmed the abnormalities and led to a consultation with a cardiologist. The cardiologist wanted my heart arteries imaged. Yikes! I seemed to have fallen into a black hole of medical referrals! I could hear the dollars evaporating from my bank account like snow sizzling on a hot wood stove. However, I dutifully bicycled seven miles to the hospital one crisp October dawn to have my arteries imaged.

At the hospital two friendly young male technicians started an IV, ran baseline tests, and injected contrast material. They also wanted to inject a medication to slow my heart rate to less than 60 beats per minute for clear images. I was pretty fit, so I suggested the medication might not be necessary. They were willing to try without the medication. Once I was inside the massive imaging machine, their smiling faces came into view around its metal flanks. "Want to know what your heart rate is now?" one asked. "Sure," I shrugged. "38 beats per minute." His grin widened. He added, "Your arteries are clear." I was relieved and a little scared. Now I had no medical reason not to try Everest.

Climbing Everest with a respected mountaineering guide company, like Adventure Consultants, is a huge financial commitment. The most highly regarded companies hire the most experienced guides and Sherpas. They pay thousands of dollars for state-of-the-art weather forecast data for the Himalayas. They supply team members with abundant food, fuel, supplemental oxygen, and other supplies. All these resources do not come cheap. And climbing permits for Everest are expensive. As with Cho Oyu, I wanted to optimize my chances for a safe climb to the summit and a safe return. I wanted to go with the best.

I asked myself, can I afford all this? Some Everest climbers mortgage their houses or take out loans. Others seek sponsors. I did not want to borrow against my home or take out a loan. I was not comfortable seeking sponsors. Who would sponsor me anyway? I was not a world-class mountaineer. I was an unknown amateur, an unimpressive looking gray-haired woman in her sixties. Besides, climbing Everest was my dream, my adventure. I did not feel comfortable asking other people to pay for it.

While I was not rich, I have been employed fulltime most of my adult life and have had a solid middle-class income. I have lived below my means and was debt free. During my 20s and 30s I saved. In my 40s I bought mutual funds to build a financial nest egg. When my aunt and mother died, I invested money they left me. I could sell some of my investments to pay for an Everest climb. Doing so would postpone retirement, but I liked my work and was not ready to retire anyway.

I had to face the fact that I could die during this climb. That was unpleasant and depressing. It would have been easier to just avoid thinking about it. Instead, I faced it head on. I updated my will and created a trust. Then, if the unthinkable happened, my sister would have an easier time with the inheritance process. Paradoxically, facing my own mortality reduced some of my anxiety about it.

Climbing Everest would require 10 weeks. I needed approval for an unpaid leave from my job. I dropped hints during informal gatherings, such as hikes with friends from work on Saturdays. My new boss, Keely Cofrin Allen, and the Executive Director of the Utah Department of Health, David Sundwall, seemed receptive, even enthusiastic. I made a formal request. Permission was granted. I had cleared another hurdle!

The Crampon-eating Crevasse

At age 61, I was a capable, though anxious, intermediate rock climber and ice climber. I had developed strategies for dealing with my fear of heights, but it was still a serious demon. I had summited a dozen peaks over 17,000 feet elevation, plus three peaks over 20,000 feet elevation. Yet I was not sure I had all the skills needed to climb Everest. I emailed Adventure Consultants and asked what I could do to further prepare myself. They suggested I take their Everest Preparation Course in New Zealand. As much as I would have liked to visit New Zealand, I could not take that much time off from work. The only company Adventure Consultants trusted to prepare me for Everest, other than themselves, was American Alpine Institute, my old friends with whom I had enjoyed several climbs in the Andes.

I arranged for training in the Mt. Baker icefall in the Cascades in July 2007. It rained the whole time Alasdair Turner, an American Alpine Institute guide, and I practiced in the icefall, a crazy maze of giant blocks of ice, crevasses (cracks in the ice), and seracs (ice towers). While trying to climb the wet rain-polished ice, I took several hard falls. Three years previously I had broken four ribs while backcountry skiing, then a year later I broke an ankle while running. Discouragement and negative self talk threatened to overwhelm me. *You're too old to be falling like this. You could break something*

– again. This is too difficult and too risky. I was tempted to quit. However, I am not a quitter. Each time I fell, I scrambled back onto my feet and tried again, trying to act more confident and enthusiastic than I felt. When I climbed to Alasdair's satisfaction, we moved on to something more difficult.

On our last morning Alasdair and I went for one more climb, an informal final exam. As the sun rose in the sky between rain showers, we climbed high into the icefall, moving well. My confidence soared. I was getting the hang of this. Near the top of the icefall, Alasdair told me to traverse up and around the corner of a steeply angled giant block of ice. I got both crampons into the smooth ice and raised my ice axe like a hammer to drive its pick into the face around the corner.

Suddenly my feet popped loose. I fell backwards and whacked the base of my skull just below my climbing helmet on a shelf of ice behind me. Pain exploded inside my head. I saw stars. As I bounced hard and continued to fall, I watched helplessly as my right crampon broke and slipped down a crevasse faster than a greased snake. I crashed onto my lower back and slid toward the crevasse that just ate my crampon. Alasdair's belay (use of friction on a climbing rope connecting him to me) jerked me to a stop. I leaned forward and peered between my bent knees into the crevasse's dark depths. I could not see the bottom. My heart ricocheted against my ribs like a panicked animal trying to escape from a cage. My inner whiner wailed, now what? How am I going to get out of this mess with only one crampon?

I took several deep breaths. Break the problem into smaller steps, I coached myself. First I needed to stand up. Pain shot through my head and back, as I sat up and tried to get my weight over my lone crampon. The wet smooth ice was very slick, so standing took several tries. Finally I rose unsteadily like a newborn foal on wobbly legs.

My crampon-less boot slipped out from under me every time I tried to take a step. I used my ice axe to chop steps, tiny ledges actually, to anchor the edge of my boot's sole. I thought of the early mountaineers who did this routinely and gained a deeper respect for what they accomplished before modern mountaineering boots and crampons. Slowly Alasdair and I picked our way through a maze of weirdly angled ice blocks and crevasses. Alasdair led, placing ice screws and clipping the rope between us as protection in case we fell. I followed, removing ice screws and slings as I climbed past them.

Finally, we reached lower-angle ice peppered with embedded gravel, which provided some traction for my crampon-less boot. My shoulders, tense with anxiety, relaxed a little. Even with the bruises and heart-pounding fright from the crampon-eating crevasse episode, I felt good about the icefall training. I had overcome self-doubt and improved my ice climbing skills. I had gotten into a desperate situation, calmed myself, and gotten out of it safely. I was ready for the next step.

Twenty Neat Stitches

My mountaineering skills and experience at altitude seemed adequate for a reasonable chance on Everest. However, the shortness of breath I had experienced high on Cho Oyu and Aconcagua was still a concern. I emailed Adventure Consultants and expressed my interest in their Everest expedition. I asked whether I could pay for additional supplemental oxygen and begin using it at 23,000 feet elevation. The answer was no. They explained that people who cannot climb to and sleep at Camp 3 at 23,500 feet elevation without supplemental oxygen do not do well higher on the mountain.

Disappointment, doubt, and indecision swirled through my head like a noxious fog. Given my history with shortness of breath and my slow pace, I could be a liability to others above 20,000 feet elevation. Do I dare risk it, I wondered. Several thoughts kept returning. This could be my last chance to do something outstanding. I don't want to die not knowing whether I could summit Everest, because I didn't try. I could always turn back, if I were putting others at unnecessary risk. Wavering between confidence and doubt, I sent my application and mountaineering resume to Adventure Consultants for their Everest 2008 expedition. Then I waited nervously for their reply.

About three weeks later, Guy Cotter, the Director of Adventure Consultants, telephoned me at home one evening. I expected he was calling to let me down gently, to tell me that Adventure Consultants was not willing to take a chance on a woman in her 60's who gets very short of breath above 20,000 feet elevation. I braced myself. Accept it with dignity, I chanted to myself, as Guy and I exchanged greetings.

Guy shifted gears and seemed to be reading from a file. "I see you started supplemental oxygen at 23,000 feet on Cho Oyu, and you fell several times during your descent." This did not sound promising. Still, I could not resist chuckling, "Jeez, no secrets from you, Guy. Yeah, I was not happy with my performance on Cho Oyu. Part of the problem was I couldn't eat or sleep very well up there."

I figured Guy was about to deliver the death blow to my Everest hopes. I expected him to say if you had trouble on Cho Oyu, you should not try Everest. Instead, he said, "I have those troubles too," with a disarming chuckle. Guy described how he sets specific goals for himself, "Right, in the next hour I will eat these three sweets and drink this bottle of water." I was touched that he would share his own vulnerabilities and secrets for managing them with me, a nobody in the mountaineering world.

Guy also suggested I hire Eric Billoud as a personal trainer. Based in New Zealand, Eric was an extreme athlete who trained others, including Everest climbers. I had never worked with a trainer before. However, in "Left for Dead," Beck Weathers wrote that his trainer got him into better shape in fewer hours of training per week than Beck could on his own. My own training program had not produced the results I wanted. I was willing to give training with Eric a try.

As Guy and I talked, I realized he had not said whether I had been accepted as a member of the Everest expedition. Timidly, I asked, "Guy, does this mean I am part of the expedition?" Guy replied, "Oh, didn't I say? Welcome aboard!" I was not sure whether to howl with joy or faint from surprise. Head spinning, I sat down on the kitchen floor. I was going to Everest!

We live in curious times. A guy in New Zealand can train an American woman he has never met via email to climb the world's highest mountain in Nepal. First, Eric asked me to describe my current training program. After reviewing it, he said it needed more speed workouts. I was surprised. I viewed climbing Everest as a test of endurance. However, if Eric said I needed speed workouts, I would do them.

I am an endurance athlete. I am slow, steady, and can go forever. I had not done anything very speedy, since I was a child. Not surprisingly, I hated Eric's speed workouts. However, I was paying him lots of money to train me, so I obediently sweated, huffed, and puffed through speed intervals on a stationary bike, increasing the intensity over the weeks. Though the dread before each speed workout never went away, I felt a grim sense of accomplishment afterwards, as I mopped up pools of sweat around the stationary bike, stripped off my drenched clothes, and showered.

Another Eric-approved training activity was a weekly hike or snowshoe carrying a 50-pound pack for several hours in the nearby mountains. On the Saturday of Thanksgiving weekend, I loaded my pack and took a short steep hike in the Wasatch foothills with some friends from work. After about an hour they turned back, while I carried on. "Be careful," were their parting words. Hey, it's me, I thought confidently. What could happen?

During my descent, I slipped on gravel and fell hard on my right elbow. It felt like a minor scrape, annoying but no big deal. I got back on my feet and continued more carefully down to the trailhead. Then I noticed large splats of fresh blood on my hiking pants. Ick! I must have done more damage than I realized. I could not see the tip of my elbow, which seemed to be the source of the bleeding. Back at my car, I cleaned up as best as I could, using tap water and paper towels at a trail head restroom. I made an X bandage over my elbow with two large Band-Aids and drove over the Wasatch Mountains to meet another set of friends in Park City to snowshoe higher in the mountains.

As I approached Park City 40 minutes later, I noticed blood on my car's armrest. "Damn!" I snarled, as I pulled over. My X bandage was saturated with blood and falling off. Half laughing and half swearing at the absurd situation, I made a cowboy bandage with a ratty old bandana, pulling it tight with one end between my teeth. I wiped the blood from my car's armrest and hoped it would not stain the pale honey-tan fabric.

My friend, Cheryl Soshnik, who was leading the snowshoe hike, was a trauma nurse. I drove to her house, hoping she could do a better job of bandaging my elbow. After greetings and hugs, Cheryl sat me down at her kitchen table and appraised my injury with cool professionalism. "You need stitches," she said evenly. My heart sank. "Does that mean I can't snowshoe with you guys?" I whimpered. Cheryl paused. I was not sure whether she was questioning my sanity, assessing my grit, or just puzzled. Then she replied, "You can come with us, if you promise to get stitches no later than tonight." I sighed with happy relief. I was keen to spend time with my friends and finish my pack-carrying workout.

After several hours of snowshoeing, we soaked in Cheryl's hot tub. Cheryl, good trauma nurse that she is, repeatedly reminded me to keep my injured elbow out of the water. By evening my elbow, forearm, and fingers were painfully swollen. I could not put off getting my elbow examined and stitched any longer.

At InstaCare a nice young woman physician said I had lacerated my elbow to the bone and torn a bursa. I stared at her bright, red nail polish and braced myself, as she numbed my elbow with several injections of local anesthetic. She closed the laceration with 20 neat stitches. X-rays showed no obvious fractures. She put my arm in a sling, gave me a prescription for antibiotics, and instructed me to see an orthopedic surgeon within the next few days. My elbow felt like it has been stung by a nest of hornets.

When my friends at work saw my sling, they gasped and asked whether I still planned to climb Everest. I was concerned too. If I needed surgery, I would not be able to train for awhile. I did not want to try Everest without being in top shape. However, a few days later the orthopedic surgeon said my elbow should heal without surgery as long as I did not re-injure it. Dodged another bullet, I grinned to myself.

To test whether Eric's program was preparing me adequately for high altitude, I made arrangements to climb Mount Kilimanjaro over Christmas in 2007. In Tanzania our guide, Ben Marshall, insisted we climb together as a team, no faster than the slowest person in our group. We followed the Marangu Route, which took us through several weirdly wonderful vegetation zones. The cloud forest at the start was inhabited by colobus monkeys in elegant black and white fur tuxedos. Above tree line, dense stands of giant heather towered over us. Higher still, iridescent bee eaters flitted among giant groundsel and giant lobelia. Above these Doctor Seuss plants, carpet-like arctic gardens segued into stark sculptures of barren rock, snow, and ice near the summit.

Our climb was very slow, wet, and cold. It rained every day except summit day. On summit day, it snowed. Even wearing a Gore-Tex rain suit and poncho did not keep me dry. Staying warm was impossible. Usually when I am cold, I can warm up by increasing my pace. However, our team's pace was so slow my hands became numb and useless. I shivered constantly and wanted to scream with impatience. Good practice for climbing Everest, I reminded myself. There, I may be slowest. If so, I hope others will be patient with me.

Ben's strategy paid off. All seven team members summited together, including a 68-year-old diabetic man. We all were delighted with our accomplishment. In contrast to the crushing fatigue and nausea I had experienced 35 years previously on Mt. Kenya and Kilimanjaro, this time was a breeze. Eric's training program seemed to be working. Encouraged, I returned home and resumed training with a vengeance.

Know When to Hold 'Em and
Know When to Fold 'Em

My only close living relative, my younger sister, Linda, seemed to hate my climbing. Perhaps she found me embarrassingly unconventional. As a shy nerdy teen, I did not wear makeup, obsess about clothes, or date boys. As a young adult I became a scientist instead of getting married and working at a more lady-like occupation. Now I climbed big mountains. Perhaps she became upset, because she worried about me and blamed me for making her worry. These were my best guesses, as we did not talk about it. I did not like upsetting my sister, but I wanted to be all I could be.

I did not look forward to telling Linda about Everest. It would be easier to not tell her or to email or write her a letter, but that seemed cowardly. I phoned her in Albuquerque, New Mexico, where she lives. When she picked up the phone, I babbled inanely about how happy I was to be accepted as a member of the Adventure Consultants Everest 2008 Expedition. I added that if I died during the climb, she would be set for life with what she would inherit from me, and if I did not die, then there would be nothing to worry about. Stupid things to say, I scolded myself, as I ran out of words. At first, Linda did not say anything. Then she replied stiffly, "You're a grown woman, it's up to you." Her response was chilly, but at least it was not explosive anger or a guilt trip. I was relieved and grateful.

Two months before I was to leave for the Everest climb, two colleagues requested a meeting with our boss and me. I expected a planning meeting for my ten-week absence. Instead it turned into a grievance session about my work. They claimed I was writing "unauthorized reports," doing other people's work, and had missed a deadline six months ago. At first, I was confused. I understood developing new reports to be part of my job. I apologized for inconvenience due to the missed deadline. My apology was bluntly rejected. Our boss seemed to be as stunned as I was. She did not side with my complaining colleagues, but she did not defend me.

I felt betrayed then angry. After the meeting, I could not stay in the building, or I would explode. I took a long walk along the nearby Jordan River. I did not want to go back to work. I did not want to have to see those people again ever. I imagined magically fast forwarding my life to being in Nepal and starting my Everest climb.

In the past, I had stayed too long in bad situations, both professional and personal. When I was denied tenure, I chose to work for the university another year, while they searched for my replacement. At the time that seemed to be my best option, a year to figure out my next career. However, it was hell working with people who had "voted me off the island." I had also stayed too long in personal relationships, hoping the guy would eventually love me as much as I loved him. I never wanted to do that again to myself. Now, when I leave a relationship, whether it is personal or professional, it is for good.

As I walked, I struggled with my roiling emotions and tried to think clearly. Have I really been "voted off the island" this time, or was this something we could fix? I knew walking away from my current job would be unprofessional and could haunt the rest of my employed life. Even if I resigned today, I would need to work through my two-week notice and see those people every day. If I had to do that anyway, perhaps I should take a few more days to think this through. As furious as I was, I might feel differently in a few days.

I gritted my teeth and went back to work that day. My boss, Keely Cofrin Allen, very generously allowed me to take my time, even until after the Everest climb, to decide whether to leave or stay. I thanked her for her generosity and acknowledged that preparing for the Everest climb had probably been more stressful to me, as well as my colleagues, than I had realized. I had not always been at my best at work. I had been impatient and irritable, especially during long meetings, when I had so much work to do before I left for Everest. My colleagues' complaints had stirred up some of my old demons about being denied tenure, and I had over-reacted. All in all, I would rather work with people who fight over who gets to do the work than with less dedicated colleagues. One of life's tough lessons is learning when to stick with something through a difficult spell and when to walk away, whether it is a job, a relationship, or a big mountain.

The drama was not over. I was in the midst of my last and most difficult weeks of fitness training. One stormy morning on the way to work, I experienced considerable chest pain, which radiated into my jaws and down my left arm. My breath came in sharp little gasps. It's probably nothing, I tried to reassure myself. However, these were classic symptoms of a heart attack. My father had died of his second heart attack at age 60, younger than I was. As a public health professional, I knew what I should do. I would feel like a fool if my symptoms were not serious, but I would be a bigger fool, if they really indicated a heart attack. I could see the headlines, "Utah Department of Health epidemiologist ignores heart attack symptoms and dies."

I went to a nearby hospital and was admitted to the Emergency Department. Nurses started an IV and a nasal cannula for oxygen. I need to practice using supplemental oxygen anyway for the upper part of the Everest climb, but this drill is unexpected, I tried to humor myself.

Technicians took a blood sample to look for heart attack enzymes and performed an EKG. Then they left. I was instructed to wait in bed for the results. My low resting heart rate kept setting off an alarm. The first couple of times the technicians responded in emergency mode. Then they ignored the alarm. I fussed and fidgeted. I should be at work. I should be training. I should be doing one of the many tasks I need to do before leaving the country for ten weeks.

Time crawled by. I was bored. At least I could read the work-related materials in my book bag. I tried to reach my bag, which was on the floor, without getting out of the hospital bed or tangling my oxygen and IV lines. It was more challenging than I expected. One of the technicians found me twisted like a pretzel, snarled in my lines, trying to keep my bare behind covered with the inadequate hospital gown, feeling ridiculous. The technician and I chuckled, as he untangled me and got my book bag for me.

Several hours later, a doctor told me my tests showed no signs of a heart attack. I was relieved yet annoyed. Such a waste of time and money! Now I would receive a whopping big bill for tests that said I was fine. Trying to soothe my crankiness on my way to work, I told myself I did the right thing.

The Mountain Is Closed

Twelve days before I was scheduled to fly to Kathmandu, Guy Cotter telephoned me from New Zealand. "This whole thing may be off. The entire mountain is closed," he said, his voice cracking, as though he were about to cry. As part of the build up to the 2008 Summer Olympics, a Chinese team of climbers was taking the Olympic Torch to the summit of Everest from the Tibet side. Chinese officials did not want to risk any chance of protesters disrupting the torch relay and closed the Tibet side of Everest. Officials from the Nepalese Ministry of Tourism claimed they did not want to jeopardize their friendly relationship with China and had closed their side of Everest. Guy added that he would fly to Kathmandu and try to persuade the Nepalese Ministry of Tourism to let us climb Everest in the spirit of the Olympics.

I tried to sound reasonable and understanding as I talked with Guy, because he sounded so upset, but I did not feel reasonable or understanding. I felt like I would explode with frustration. After 11 years of developing skills for the climb of a lifetime, now it would not happen. I could not imagine postponing the climb another year. I was not sure I could put myself through another year of the most rigorous physical training of my life. Though I had paid for travel insurance, I was not sure I would get any of my money back. Paying for another chance to climb Everest seemed out of reach, as did getting another unpaid leave for 10 weeks.

Over the following days the news was scary and depressing. Violent demonstrations sprang up around the world protesting the Chinese occupation of Tibet. The Dalai Lama threatened to resign his leadership of exiled Tibetans. Climbing Everest seemed frivolous in comparison, but I still felt sorry for myself.

Friends from the Wasatch Mountain Club were planning a farewell potluck dinner for me. Instead of looking forward to it, I felt dull and discouraged. I would have to tell them the climb would not happen. When I arrived at the condominium clubhouse where the dinner was being held, my work colleague and outdoor friend, Dave Rabiger, was hanging a string of bright Himalayan prayer flags across the fire place. I sadly told him Everest was closed. He looked confused. I tried to explain Guy's phone call, as a few more friends arrived and gathered around. "They can't do that!" they protested indignantly. I replied wearily, "They can do whatever they want. Things don't work over there the way they do here." Their indignation touched me. I shrugged and said to Dave, "Go ahead and hang the prayer flags. They can't hurt."

As the flags went up, my spirits lifted. My friends were throwing a party for me. I was not going thank them by being negative. They had knocked themselves out and prepared a feast. After dinner, I slipped into the bathroom and put on my huge down pants and parka, massive three-layer plastic Millet mountaineering boots, balaclava, and ski goggles. I glanced in the mirror. I looked like a Teletubby from Mars. I burst out laughing. I staggered comically out of the bathroom making Darth Vader sounds, fighting an imaginary head wind. My friends looked at me uncertainly. Then they giggled, crowded around, and bombarded me with questions. The guys particularly were fascinated by the design of my mountaineering boots and the many pockets and zippers of my down parka and pants. Their excitement and interest in my adventure surprised and moved me. I was glad I did not let discouragement about the closure of Everest spoil this lovely evening with friends.

After the farewell potluck, I alternated between immobilizing anxiety and bursts of frantic activity. I made last minute arrangements for being away, knowing I might have to cancel them. Dave Rabiger hung the string of prayer flags from the farewell potluck dinner outside my cube at work. Dave had climbed glaciated peaks in South America, had some close calls, and knew the dangers first hand. Those bright little flags were a ray of hope. I went to International Mountain Equipment and paid for my special-order down sleeping bag rated to minus 40 degrees. The lean wiry climbers who ran the shop had been graciously holding the bag for me, pending further news about whether we would be allowed to climb Everest. They grinned and wished me luck. I needed it.

Several days after Guy's phone call, I received email from Adventure Consultants. The Nepalese Ministry of Tourism still had not issued our climbing permit, but Guy instructed us to fly to Kathmandu, as though we would be allowed to climb. Time sped up and slowed down unpredictably. Sometimes I feared I would never get everything done, before I left home. Other times, the days seemed to drag on endlessly, and the departure date would never come. I did my hardest workouts then tapered my training for the last few days, giving my body time to recover. I put the finishing touches on my gear, like zipper pull tabs I could operate while wearing big gloves. I checked and rechecked my piles of gear against my equipment lists. I squashed everything into two large duffle bags and two carry-ons. I was as ready as I could be.

Lift Off

March 26. Even with the marvels of modern travel, getting from Utah to Kathmandu took three days of long flights interspersed with additional long hours of waiting in airports. After the short flight from Salt Lake, I clumped through the Los Angeles International airport wearing my red and black Millet mountaineering boots, waiting for the midnight flight across the Pacific to Hong Kong. Though the boots were heavy, hot, and made walking awkward, they would be the most difficult piece of equipment to replace if lost, so I wore them. I got plenty of stares. One grandmotherly woman asked whether I was going river rafting. River rafting? Then she said her son enjoyed river rafting. Apparently she was proud of him and welcomed an excuse to talk about him.

Later, two tall young guys asked me to settle a bet. "Are your boots for skiing or mountaineering?" one asked with a friendly grin.

"Mountaineering," I grinned back.

"I win!" he said to his friend. "Where are you headed?"

"Everest."

"Hiking?"

"No, I will try for the summit."

"Awesome! Good luck!" We shook hands. The interest of friendly strangers helped distract me from worry about the closure of the mountain. Their encouragement reminded me of how much attitudes toward women mountaineers have changed in recent years.

After the long night flight across the Pacific, I enjoyed doing yoga in the nearly deserted new airport in Hong Kong. As the sun rose, rain clouds turned smoky orange, then peach, then pale gold.

The next day, during one of my walks up and down the aisles during the flight to Kathmandu, another passenger named Brian remembered me from Aconcagua in early 2007. Brian had climbed Everest a few months afterwards. At 21,000 feet elevation, he developed high altitude pulmonary edema, a life threatening condition, and had to descend to Pheriche, which is at 14,000 feet elevation. He lost 30 lbs. After about 10 days he felt better. He and a guide, Willie Benegas, then climbed back up and summited. He was back with his wife and two young daughters to share a little of his Everest experience with them.

Brian's accomplishments were impressive and intimidating. I wondered whether I would get seriously sick like him. Would I even get a chance to try for the summit with the current closure of Everest? Questions wheeled like vulture through my mind. I firmly told them to leave. I had prepared as well as I could. Some things, like closure of the mountain, were beyond my control. Worrying about them would not help.

In Kathmandu at last, the lines for baggage claim, customs, passport stamps, and visa approval were as convoluted as I remembered from previous visits. In the crowd, I could hear French, German, Italian, Spanish, Japanese, Chinese, and various Nepalese languages. I was part of the international community of tourists drawn to Nepal. It was exciting and exhausting, especially after three days of travel with little sleep. I collected my duffle bags at baggage claim and threaded my teetering cart through customs then through crowds of eager porters and taxi drivers vying for my business.

I spotted a small neatly dressed Nepali man with an Adventure Consultants sign. He and two wiry little porters grabbed my bags and rushed through the airport parking lot to a van. As I tipped them, a third man asked, "Something for me?" I was not sure whether he had helped with my duffels or not. I gave him a dollar. He looked at it sadly for several seconds. When he concluded that I was not going to give him more, he disappeared into the shadows. The night air was mild and pleasant. It felt wonderful to be outside after three days of flights and airports.

As the driver wove through a confusing maze of narrow, dark streets, I noticed how quiet and empty Kathmandu seemed. During previous visits, it had teemed with crowds even late at night. Tonight we passed only a few small groups of soldiers in camouflage uniforms with automatic weapons and one family, a mother in her best sari and two small girls in frilly dresses. I wondered where they were going so late in their finery. The contrast between the vulnerable little family and the armed soldiers was a chilling reminder of the tense political climate and protests about the Chinese occupation of Tibet.

At Hotel Shanker, a tiny aged porter, his face as brown and creased as well worn leather, insisted on wrangling all of my bags, which taken together weighed more than I did. I helped him cram them into a crotchety elevator then we hauled them into my room. I gave him $3. His lined face beamed as he bowed his thanks and left. My room smelled like musty old wood, reminding me of my grandmother's basement in Kansas. As I settled in bed for the night, party music squawked from a nearby bar. Tired but too wound up to sleep, I read for a couple of hours. Finally I slept from 2 am until 6 am, my longest sleep in four days.

March 29. I got up, dressed, and found the breakfast buffet in the hotel. It included an eye-popping array of local fruits and juices, hot and cold cereals, yogurt, sausage, bacon, eggs, potatoes, curry dishes, rolls, muffins, toast, butter, jam, tea and coffee. A smiling Nepalese chef offered to prepare a made-to-order omelet. This spread was far more opulent than my usual breakfast of oatmeal, sliced banana, and soy drink. I especially enjoyed the fresh papayas, mangos, pineapple, watermelon, and Asian pears.

As I was eating, I saw Mike Roberts, our expedition leader, enter the dining room. I waved. He joined me at a table near a window. Mike looked as fit and strong as when we had met three years ago on Cho Oyu.

"Hey, Mike, you and I have the same haircuts," I joked, as I ran a hand over my closely cropped hair, while he sat down opposite me. I had my hair cut very short before this trip figuring haircut opportunities would be scarce on Everest. Mike eyed me warily and replied, "I don't know what that means."

"Neither do I," I laughed, feeling awkward. I tried again. "How are you? How's your wife?"

"I'm divorced now," Mike answered in a tone that was hard to read. Though I had talked to hundreds of divorced people for my research as a university professor, I never knew quite what to say in social situations. I'm sorry? Congratulations? Mike said the divorce was sad but amicable. Trying to sound reassuring, I said being married must be difficult for a mountain guide because of all the time apart. From the look on Mike's face, it was not the right thing to say. I'm batting a thousand today, I thought ruefully. Mike and I finished breakfast while talking about cameras and photography in the mountains, a safer topic, as he is a terrific photographer.

After breakfast I left the hotel on foot, saying "no thanks" to several rickshaw and taxi guys. Though the smog was worse than anything I had experienced at home and pedestrians must be nimble to avoid being run over, I wanted to walk. I exchanged U.S. dollars for Nepalese rupees, bought bottled water at the Blue Bird grocery store, and found an Internet place to send email to my sister and friends.

On my walk back to the hotel two boys in their school uniforms fell into step along side me and chatted me up in good English. Though this was fun, I knew what was coming from previous trips to Kathmandu. They chattered, "We don't want money, Misses. Money make people crazy. You like children, Misses? Children need milk. Buy us milk, Mama." Though it sounded innocent enough, it worked like this. The boys would take tourists to the grocery store, the tourists would buy them a carton of milk at an inflated price, after the tourist and boys would part company, the boys would take the unopened carton back to the store and get a cut of the profits. I replied, "No, thanks. You guys speak really good English. Keep studying in school and you will do well." When they saw I was not going to buy any milk for them, they drifted back into the throngs of pedestrians, no doubt looking for more gullible -- or more generous -- tourists. I felt a mixture of shame and annoyance, shame that I was too stingy to buy the kids milk, even if they were scamming me, and annoyance about being treated like a bottomless wallet instead of a human being. Walking the streets of Kathmandu sometimes felt like being bitten to death by ducks, ducks who are just trying to survive.

The Everest Team

March 30. Our first expedition meeting was before dinner. I felt shy, when I found our meeting room at the hotel. Several fit lean climbers were milling around. They were probably my team mates and guides. I would spend the next two months with these people. Would we get along?

After we introduced ourselves, Mike gave a Power Point overview of the hike to Base Camp and the climb. His eyes rolled like those of a startled horse. I could only imagine the pressure he must have felt. Besides the usual uncertainties and dangers of climbing Everest, we still had no climbing permit due to the closure of the mountain. There was a good chance we would not be allowed to climb. When my anxiety began to career out of control, I remembered Mike's advice during the Cho Oyu climb. Don't think about the summit. Think about what you need to do in the next five minutes, in the next hour, and where you need to be at the end of the day. Right now I needed to listen to Mike's overview of our Everest climb and get to know my fellow climbers.

We were an expedition of eight climbers, four guides, 18 climbing Sherpas, and 10 camp Sherpas. In age, we spanned five decades, with climbers in their 20s, 30s, 40s, 50s, and 60s. Unlike many of my previous mountaineering trips, I was not the only woman. Two mothers and their daughters, Cheryl and Nikki Bart from Australia and Roxanne and Robyn Faike from the United States, were vying to become the first mother-daughter team to summit Everest together. Nor was I the oldest climber. Hedd-wyn (pronounced "Heth-win") Williams, an oral facial surgeon from Calgary, was three months older than I. He crowed triumphantly, when we made this discovery. I joked about not being able to play the "woman card" or the "age card."

Hedd-wyn was a wiry animated guy about my size. He reminded me of an energetic elf with white hair and a white beard. He described his many ice climbs in Canada, even his injuries and accidents, with great enthusiasm. Phil Drowley was a police sergeant from the Isle of Man. Steve Novick, originally from Wisconsin, was living in London, and had a background in international finance. Both Phil and Steve were tall and looked fit. Cheryl, a corporate attorney, and her daughter, Nikki, a third-year medical student, were both trim, about my size, and brilliantly blond, as were Roxi from Nevada and her daughter, Robyn, from Colorado.

Everyone had impressive experience. Both mother-daughter teams had climbed the other Seven Summits, the highest peak on each of the seven continents. Hedd-wyn had summited Ama Dablam, a stunningly beautiful icy pinnacle over 22,000 feet in elevation, which we would pass during our hike to Everest Base Camp. Phil had climbed high on Everest previously. This time he hoped to become the first person from the Isle of Man to summit. Steve had completed an Iron Man and lost part of his thumb to cancer. Clearly, each of my team mates had met serious challenges and overcome them. I just hoped I could keep up.

Our guides were also impressive. Mike Roberts has guided for over 20 years, primarily in Antarctica, the Himalayas, and New Zealand. This would be his third time on Everest. Lydia Bradey was tall, willowy, and very toned. In 1988, she became the first woman to summit Everest without supplemental oxygen. Victor Saunders was dark, wiry, and sometimes mistaken for a Sherpa. He had done many difficult ascents around the world and had published books about them. Ang Dorje Sherpa was one of two Sherpas who tried to reach Rob Hall high on Everest in 1996 during the horrific storm that claimed Hall's life along with so many others. Ang Dorje had summited Everest eleven times.

Lhakpa Dorje Sherpa, Phu Tashi Sherpa, and I remembered each other from Cho Oyu and exchanged shy greetings. For dinner we all went to the Roadhouse in Thamel by taxi to avoid crowds agitated by the Tibet troubles. I overcame my shyness and chatted with the other climbers seated near me. Cheryl kidded me about my "stage name," SilverFox, which I had adopted a few years ago to counteract my anxiety about aging. "One can always use a good fox," she teased. I started calling her and Nikki Golden Fox Number 1 and Golden Fox Number 2, a gentle reference to their being pretty, blond, and clever.

Several hikers would accompany us for the hike to Everest Base Camp. They would be led by Mark Sedon, one of my guides on Cho Oyu, and Mark Morrison, another guide, whose wife, Laurel, would be our Everest Base Camp manager. Among the hikers was Sue, a blond, middle-aged woman from South Africa. She and I had met soon after our arrival in Kathmandu. We had shared a taxi and guide to see the nearby village of Bhaktapur and had bought digital cameras together in Thamel. Eduardo, a bear-like orthopedic surgeon from Mexico, was about my age. He enthusiastically told us that he had summited six of the Seven Summits and had climbed almost to the summit of Everest some years ago. Two of Phil's policemen friends, Peter and Dave, and Hedd-wyn's friend as well as his orthopedic surgeon, Hugh, also were among our hikers to Base Camp.

Suddenly, I wished my sister, Linda, were here. It would be so cool to share the hike to Base Camp with her. However, Linda does not like to hike. In spite of that, several years ago, she had arranged for us to take ranger guided tours of restricted parts of Carlsbad Caverns. Though she was sometimes out of her comfort zone, she did well with the climbing and crawling. Not many sisters, then in their 50s, share such adventures. I will treasure those cave excursions with my sister for the rest of my life.

Lukla

April 1. Before dawn we met in the Hotel Shanker lobby for an early flight to Lukla, a village at 9,200 feet elevation, where we would begin walking toward Everest Base Camp. We still did not have a climbing permit, so Mike stayed in Kathmandu to wait in line at the Ministry of Tourism, where the permits usually were issued. I wondered wryly whether flying on April Fools' Day was a good idea, given the frequency of flight cancellations due to poor visibility, occasional plane crashes, and the fact we still did not have a climbing permit.

After a lot of hurrying up and waiting at the Kathmandu Airport, we boarded a small plane. A Nepalese flight attendant gave each of us a single piece of hard candy and a small wad of cotton for our ears. At 7:30 am, the little plane shuddered down the runway, climbed out of the haze over Kathmandu, and soared over terraced farms and villages, rivers and forested hills. As we soared toward the Himalayas, I thought I caught a glimpse of Everest's summit just before it disappeared in a swirl of clouds. After a half hour, our plane wheeled, lined up with a tiny airstrip below, and went into a sharp dive, a roller coaster fan's dream. The landing was hard, and the braking was sharp. As we lurched to a stop, I noticed I was gripping my arm rests with white knuckles.

We deplaned into cold swirling mist. I hunched my shoulders against the damp and hoped we would start walking soon, so I could warm up. Our guides herded us from the airstrip to the nearby Northfield Lodge for breakfast. Meanwhile, our Sherpas collected our duffels of hiking gear and organized porters to carry them to Phakding, where we would stay tonight. Our climbing gear was being transported by truck, then by yak train, and would arrive at Base Camp about the same time we would. After a breakfast of eggs and Tibetan fry bread, we shouldered our daypacks and started our eleven-day walk to Base Camp. It was only about 45 miles and 8,400 feet of elevation gain, but a leisurely pace would give our bodies time to acclimatize.

We set out on Lukla's cobblestone paths and joined the steady stream of climbers, hikers, local people, thin little Himalayan ponies and dzos (yak-cow hybrids). We hiked past stone tea houses, lodges, shops, and homes amid a patchwork of hand-tilled fields. Any patch of arable land was bordered by rock walls and was either growing something, or families were preparing for planting with hand tools. Everything moved on the backs of lean little ponies, dzos, or porters. Some porters carried impossibly large loads that weighed more than they did. From the back they looked like loads that had sprouted legs. Hedd-wyn joked that he wanted his day pack to sprout legs like that and carry itself.

Stone benches built into village walls along the path provided porters with a convenient place to prop their huge loads and rest. At one of these benches, I asked a porter, who was smaller than me, if I could try to lift and carry his load. With a shy smile, he helped me steady his unwieldy carrying basket, while I got under it and lifted it by straightening my legs. I staggered as the load threatened to pull me over backwards. I managed to take about 20 awkward steps, trying not to trip in the rocky path or step in piles of dzo dung. The wiry little men and women who carry such loads had my undying respect.

As we walked, I saw no cars, motor bikes, bicycles, carts, or wheel barrows. The cobbled paths were good, but they were too rocky and had too many steep steps for anything with wheels. Most people walked. A few wealthier Sherpas rode tough little ponies with bright red saddle blankets and jingling bells on their bridles. Porters carried expedition supplies as well as hand-sawn wooden beams and sheets of plywood to construction sites several days' walk up the valley. I felt as though I had stepped back into Tolkien's Middle Earth. Then I would pass a porter wearing a baseball cap and listening to an iPod. We were still in the 21st century.

We each hiked at our own pace, taking in the sights. Children ran from the doorways of village houses to greet us with "'Allo" or "Namaste" (a greeting that means roughly "the best in me greets the best in you, and when we are in that place, we are one," and often accompanied by hands in a prayer position.) Some children patiently posed for photographs. Others held out wild flowers to us. Unlike the kids in Kathmandu, no one asked us for money. After a couple of hours, we stopped at a lodge for lemon or black tea. Then we hit the trail again.

We passed Russell Brice, who has guided climbers to Everest's summit from the Tibet side for years. Because of the closure of Tibet to all climbers and hikers, he was on the Nepal side this season. I had met Russell on Cho Oyu, but he did not remember me. I told him I had learned a lot from the documentary, "Everest: Beyond the Limit, Season 1" which featured his 2006 expedition on Everest. He gave me a pained look. Perhaps he did not like the documentary's portrayal of his expedition. Or maybe he just did not want to talk to anyone just then.

We arrived in Phakding around 1:30 pm. After lugging our duffels to our rooms in the lodge and eating lunch, some of us hiked above the village to the local monastery. It had been recently refurbished and had lovely tapestries, Buddhist statues, and thankhas (religious paintings). I sat and meditated for a few minutes in the cool dark interior. The view from outside the monastery could have inspired stories about Shangri-la. Back at the lodge, my room overlooked a partly harvested patch of bok choy, reminding me that growing food in this part of the world requires a lot of back-breaking work.

Namche

April 2. Fueled by omelets, toast, jam, and tea, we were hiking by 8 am. We passed through thickets of rhododendrons with bright red clusters of flowers, magnolia-like trees with large white blossoms, and something that looked like mountain laurel, whose blooms resembled tiny Japanese lanterns. Small purple primroses carpeted stream banks and hillsides. Dark birds, the size of a small crow with an orange beak and a long speckled tail, swooped across our path. Strings of prayer flags of red, blue, green, white, and yellow fluttered from flag poles. We passed walls of mani stones carved with Buddhist prayers, passing them on our right. We passed a stream-powered prayer wheel, waiting for the spring thaw to power its paddles. I felt as though I was walking through a beautiful dream.

As we climbed steeper sections of the trail, I carefully passed several pack trains of laden dzos. They were mellower than their yak relatives, but I still respected their long sharp horns. One dzo swung its head as I passed it and snagged me with its horn, bruising my shoulder. It seemed to have been an accident rather than an aggressive act, so we parted peacefully.

As I hiked, I fell into conversation with Emmy, a tall young woman from Idaho. She was hiking to Everest Base Camp then on to Island Peak. A rugged looking middle-aged Australian guy had planned to attempt Everest from the Tibet side, but he changed at the last minute to the Nepal side after the Chinese closure of Tibet.

I hiked to the gate for Sagarmatha National Park and waited for the others. Ang Dorje found me and sent me back to Kailash Lodge, a walk of about 20 or 30 minutes, for lunch with the others. I felt a bit silly. During our expedition overview in Kathmandu, Mike had warned us about getting too far ahead. I gratefully ate the fried rice Laurel, our base camp manager, had thoughtfully ordered for me. Ordering meals in local lodges often is a complicated and time consuming process.

After lunch, we hiked through more rugged terrain than yesterday. The gorges were deeper, and the Dudh Kosi (Milk River) churned and boiled more fiercely under the swaying suspension bridges we crossed. The bridges bounced and bucked under foot, until I found the right rhythm and length of stride to cushion the bounce. The bridges teamed with climbers, hikers, porters and dzos carrying loads, Himalayan ponies and their riders. I felt like part of a traveling international circus.

After another suspension bridge, we climbed a long steep hill toward Namche, the main trading center in the Khumbu region. Pack trains of dzos churned up choking clouds of dust, which coated my sweat-drenched face and shirt. Armed guards stopped me on a high dusty traverse before the last stretch into Namche. I waited about half an hour for the others. Lydia, Victor, and Ang Dorje caught up, and we walked confidently past the young guards, who were then busy chatting amongst themselves. When we were perhaps 50 yards past them, they shouted at us. We still did not have our climbing permit. This could mean trouble. Ang Dorje imperiously said something in Sherpa and waved a paper, which could have been the bill from our lunch. The guards waved us on. It was good to have a famous Sherpa like Ang Dorje to smooth over situations like this.

We entered Namche, a large village of white stone rectangular buildings with blue roofs. The tink, tink, tink of stone masons' hammers followed us as we wove through narrow paths toward the center of town, where we would stay at the Khumbu Lodge for the next few days. We climbed up steep stairs and checked in. My room in the basement was very dark and cold, so I read in the upstairs dining room near a sunny window. After sunset the temperature plummeted, so I joined others on low stools around a yak dung stove in the center of the room. The stove was surprisingly warm and not smoky or stinky.

The next day I went for a stroll through Namche Bazaar downhill from our lodge. Along a steep cobbled path, shops and stalls overflowed with down parkas, sleeping bags, T-shirts, ball caps, hiking boots, maps, and souvenirs, both Chinese made and locally made. I particularly liked the carved wooden T-shaped braces porters used as a walking stick while carrying their loads and as a seat while resting.

However, my heart was set on a yak bell. While hiking the past couple of days, I had enjoyed listening to the mellow clong clitty clong of bells Sherpas put around their lead dzo's necks. At the Bazaar, I shook several yak bells gently. They sounded tinny and harsh and looked factory made. I wanted a bell of hand-beaten metal with a traditional yak-hair collar and a rich mellow tone.

I found one I liked. A small local woman wearing a traditional Sherpani jacket, skirt and apron beamed at me from behind her counter. "How much?" I asked. She named a price. "Too much," I replied, as I put the bell down and started to walk away. "You make offer," she said with an eager grin. I remembered bargaining was part of a tradition of gamesmanship in this part of the world. I made a low offer. She shook her head cheerfully, "Too low." We went back and forth for a few minutes. Usually I dislike bargaining, but her obvious enjoyment was contagious. I made a final offer and stuck to it in spite of her spirited urging to offer more. We shook hands on an agreed-upon price. I paid her and started to leave with my bell. She plucked my sleeve and said, "Missy, you give me too much. I no feel good inside. Others take your money. Not me. No good, no good," she said earnestly, patting her stomach. I realized she was correct. I had misread my rupee notes and overpaid her.

This local woman's honesty deeply moved me. Though she did not look poor, no doubt she was less well off than I and would have liked to keep the over-payment. She did not have to correct a foreign tourist who surely seemed fabulously rich to her. With tears in my eyes, I thanked her for her honesty and gave her back most of the overpayment. She grinned warmly and bowed, taking my right hand in both of hers. This small exchange in broken English, smiles, and gestures underscored a universal sense of ethics that can transcends culture and economic status.

Later than evening, our expedition leader, Mike, caught up with us in Namche. He had our climbing permit at last. Perhaps the issuing of permits meant the restrictions on climbing Everest had ended. I felt relieved and optimistic.

April 3. Today we took an acclimatization hike above Namche. As we climbed, we could look down on the village, which looked like a giant horseshoe of white stone buildings with blue roofs curving around a deep ravine. We climbed above tree line past wind-tortured juniper along a blustery ridge to the Everest View Lodge, where we stopped for tea and had our first views of Everest's summit. It was exciting to see our goal, visible and tangible, yet too far away to be scary.

As we hiked on to a local hospital in Kunde established by Sir Edmund Hillary, clouds rolled in, and snow showers pelted us. We wanted to see inside the hospital, but it was closed. A few local patients were waiting on the stone patio outside. One barefoot woman seemed to have a painful condition involving all her toes, which looked abnormally pale. Hedd-wyn thought it might be frostbite, but Simon Jensen, our expedition physician, and Hugh, an orthopedic surgeon, were not so sure. I find health-related matters fascinating and enjoyed listening to their lively discussion.

We hiked through swirling snowflakes to the Khumjung Bakery in a small barren village and ducked inside to the warmth of a yak dung stove and a variety of pies and pastries. After our break, we headed through more small villages back to Namche. Small boys and girls raced along stone paths, their joyous energy at odds with the drab brown villages. Some kids carried child-sized wooden pack frames for carrying the stone blocks chiseled by their parents. Hugh said parents value their children according to how much they can carry. Because everything must move on the backs of people or pack animals, this kind of "currency" was understandable, yet Hugh said carrying heavy loads can stunt children's growth. As enchanting as I found hiking through these villages, Hugh's remarks reminded me that life is hard for many Sherpas, even with the influx of modern clothing and gadgets.

Greetings and Blessings

April 4. We left Namche early. After a long uphill hike through altitude-stunted trees and rhododendrons, we arrived in time for prayers at Tengboche's beautiful monastery. Afterwards, we had pizza and our choice of bakery goodies, including lemon pie and apple pie, at a local lodge. The pizza had less cheese and the pie was less sweet than I expected, but they were pretty good. Back on the trail, we passed local men who were making improvements on the trail using well worn hand tools, noticeably improving it. I put 100 rupees in their donation box and thanked them for their work. They grinned and namasted energetically.

April 5. At 8:30 am we left the crowded little lodge in Deboche where we had slept last night. Light snow was falling, and a brisk breeze shredded mist into streamers, adding a hint of mystery to the rugged landscape. The rhododendrons, draped in Spanish moss, stone walls, houses, and even yaks, wore lacy garlands of new snow. During one of our rest breaks, a local horseman galloped up the trail and clattered past us, his pony's harness bells jangling shrilly. I wished I had the heart and lungs of that tough little pony at this altitude. At about 12,000 feet elevation, I was beginning to notice the effects of thin air.

We slipped and slid on snowy trails to Pangboche. First we went to Ang Dorje's mother's house. We sat in a large room in her traditional Sherpa home on long narrow benches covered with wool Tibetan carpets, our backs to a wall of windows. Across from the benches, large shelves and wooden cabinets with glass doors were full of huge brass pots, quilts, and blankets. Pictures of her famous son, other climbers, and Buddhist rimpoches (spiritual teachers) decorated the walls. Ang Dorje's mother solemnly shook hands with each of us and poured us Sherpa tea, a sweet, warm mixture of black tea and milk. Ang Dorje told us that she was 79 years of age, an unusually advanced age for Sherpas who live their traditional lifestyle.

Next we found Lama Geshe's house. About 80 years of age, Lama Geshe has been blessing Everest climbers for many years. When he was younger, he hiked to Everest Base Camp to conduct Buddhist ceremonies requesting a safe climb. Now climbers come to him. Several groups were ahead of us, so we waited in the snowy courtyard, hunched against the chill. While we waited, Ang Dorje showed us how to wrap our donations properly in our katas (white scarves), which we would present to Lama Geshe.

At last it was our turn to file into the main room of Lama Geshe's home. Like Ang Dorje's mother's house, pictures of climbers and rimpoches decorated the walls. Lama Geshe sat behind a long wooden table with a wall of windows behind him, looking very round and substantial in a red puffy down jacket over his yellow robes. We sat on rows of benches covered with Tibetan-style wool carpets opposite him, while he prayed chanted prayers, seemingly oblivious to the flash and click of climbers' cameras. Periodically Ang Dorje passed a plate of raw white rice, from which we each took a generous pinch with our right hand. Ang Dorje signaled when we were supposed to toss the rice during the ceremony. I kept running out, so I surreptitiously swept scattered grains from the table into my right hand, hoping that I was not committing some taboo.

After the prayers and rice tossing, we lined up to present our donations wrapped in katas and receive our individual blessings. I was so nervous when I approached Lama Geshe, I started to leave before he could finish blessing me. His solemn face burst into an impish grin. His spontaneous amusement eased my embarrassment. I smiled back sheepishly and bowed, as he placed my kata and a golden thread around my neck.

After the ceremony, we hiked toward Pheriche. We had excellent views of Ama Dablam standing guard like a glistening white sentinel. Hedd-wyn happily reminisced about his climb of the peak a few years ago, for some reason calling it "Ahble Dahble". It looked steep and difficult to climb, especially at high altitude. I was impressed that he had summited it.

In the afternoon we arrived at the White Yak Lodge in Pheriche, a dusty village at 14,000 feet elevation, where we would stay for the next few days. The White Yak Lodge, like most of the lodges we had visited, used energy-saving lights and passive solar heat. Showers and laundry had to be arranged in advance, so hot water could be prepared only when it was needed. We in rich nations could learn from these Nepalese lodge managers how to share a small planet with finite resources.

After stowing our packs and duffels in our rooms upstairs, some of us sat around the yak dung stove in the dining room and traded songs. I sang "She'll be comin' 'round the mountain." Lhakpa Thundu sang "Alouette" in French. Some of the other Sherpas sang traditional Sherpa songs. Perhaps the lyrics said rude things about foreign climbers and hikers, but the melodies sounded lovely and exotic to me. Robyn sang some arias with her beautiful operatic voice. Lydia Bradey told us about climbing high on K2 and getting chased down by bad weather before she could summit. She was surprised to learn that I was 15 years older than her. I was flattered. I teasingly suggested that she and I could be the third mother daughter team of our expedition.

Pheriche and Lobuche

April 6. We awoke to more new snow. It transformed dusty drab Pheriche into a fairyland of snow-laced roof lines and stone paddock walls. After breakfast, we took an acclimatization hike through swirling snowflakes. We headed up yak paths over a couple of rocky ridges behind the White Yak Lodge, where I had gone for an evening walk last night at dusk. The falling snow made the faint trail slippery. No one wanted to twist an ankle with our big climb ahead of us, but we persisted until we gained about 1500 feet of elevation.

We saw very few dzos now. Dzos are more docile and give more milk than yaks. However, they suffer at high elevations and from cold temperatures. Pack animal handlers switch to yaks for carrying loads above 14,000 feet elevation. Yaks are more temperamental than dzos yet hardier and shaggier.

Back at the lodge, several Sherpas were sitting at a table, sharing a platter of small boiled red potatoes. The Sherpas shucked off the paper-thin skins, dipped the potatoes in a bowl of salt, and popped them into their mouths, eating with relish between bursts of animated conversation and laughter. I admired their ability to turn such a simple meal into a celebration.

I had caught the cold that was working its way through our group. At home it would have been a minor annoyance. Here, at 14,000 feet elevation, it could turn into pneumonia, which happened during one of my previous climbs in Bolivia. Simon, our expedition physician, suggested aspirin and an early night, so I crawled into my down sleeping bag upstairs. I was very congested, so I tried to sleep sitting up. Sue, one of the hikers and my roommate, kindly brought me a small pot of hot lemon tea.

April 7. By morning I felt terrible. I had not slept much. I had a raging sinus headache, both ears hurt, and my throat was very sore. I felt feverish and weak. We were supposed to be packed before breakfast for an early start for Lobuche. While packing, I felt as though I were struggling through thick mud and had to stop several times to rest. As I lugged my duffel and back pack down the narrow steep stairs, I met Mike and Mark Sedon, one of the guides for our hikers. I tried to look healthier and more cheerful than I felt. "You look a bit rough," Mark said with a sympathetic grin. Rats! I'm found out, I thought dismally. He can see that I am sick.

"You stay here today," Mike said firmly. "But I need to acclimatize," I wailed, panic rising. I was afraid that if I fell out of synch with the rest of the team's acclimatization schedule, I would not be able to climb to the summit. "If you go higher now, you'll get sicker. You have plenty of time to acclimatize, when you feel better," Mike assured me. I felt sad to be left behind as the rest of the climbers left, like a dog tied to the porch, while everyone else went off for a fine adventure. Yet I was relieved that I did not have to push myself to hike today while feeling so crummy.

Simon gave me the antibiotic, Augmentin, and a decongestant. I went back upstairs and crawled back into my sleeping bag. When I got bored, I went downstairs to the sun room, which had walls of windows looking down the valley, providing a sweeping view of the starkly beautiful valley and surrounding mountains. The sun room was toasty warm from passive solar heating and full of bright sunshine, a welcome change from my cold dark room upstairs. I propped myself up on a bench in a sunny corner with a good view and a good book, "Three Cups of Tea," by Greg Mortenson and David Oliver Relin. Morning drifted lazily into afternoon, as I listened to the wind and watched choughs (pronounced "chuffs"), dark birds resembling small crows, soar in the thermals. Hikers and climbers from other expeditions came and went, sometimes pausing for tea, lunch, or rest. We resembled an old-fashioned British club, reading and dozing as the bright afternoon faded into evening.

April 8. By morning I felt much better. I was pleasantly surprised by the difference that staying an extra day at Pheriche had made. The hikers and I headed up to Lobuche with our guides, Mark Morrison and Mark Sedon. We ambled up the trail in bright sunshine. I walked awhile with Eduardo. Until today, he had cheerfully reported how good he felt and how great his appetite was. In fact, he did this so often, I wondered whether he "protested too much" and was anxious about the altitude. Today he was quiet and seemed unwell. A day later he decided to go no higher and returned to Kathmandu. How high altitude will affect people is hard to predict, even for guys like Eduardo with considerable high altitude experience.

On our way to Lobuche, we stopped at a cluster of stone monuments for climbers who had died on Everest. The monuments were scattered across a small rocky valley and overflowed up some of the surrounding ridges. It was a sad place. Dark clouds rolled in, mirroring my mood. As I wandered among the tributes to those who have died, most of whom were younger than I, my eyes burned with tears. I felt sad for lives cut short and those who grieved for the dead. My gut boiled with self-doubt. I wondered whether I had made a good choice coming here to climb Everest at 61 years of age.

After a long steady climb, we reached Lobuche at about 16,000 feet elevation. We crossed a half-frozen lake of mud and yak dung then passed a very stinky outhouse to get to the Eco Lodge, where we would stay tonight. Though Lobuche was grimmer than Pheriche, I was glad to re-unite with the climbers. I liked the hikers and enjoyed their company, but the climbers were my tribe.

April 9. My roommate, Sue, had a rough night. Neither of us got much sleep, as she coughed and gasped all night. Repeatedly, Sue's breathing would slow to a stop, then she would gasp with alarm, as her breathing suddenly resumed. Her breathing irregularities were typical of periodic breathing or Cheyne-Stokes respiration, a common symptom of moderate altitude sickness. I felt bad that Sue had caught my cold. She probably felt as lousy as I had felt a few days ago.

Sue was understandably anxious about her symptoms, so I offered to get our expedition doctor, Simon. After examining her, Simon reassured Sue that her symptoms were usual for someone who had just climbed to a higher altitude and had caught a cold. She rested, while the rest of us went for an acclimatization hike toward Everest Base Camp, then up a ridge to some weather instruments. Laurel and her husband, Mark Morrison, also had had a bad night with symptoms similar to Sue's. They hiked with us part of the way before wisely deciding to go back to the lodge.

Some of us continued on to the Pyramid International Research Center. One of the researchers gave us a tour, a special treat for me as a former researcher. One dusty lab included several battered exercise bikes for studies of high altitude physiology. Naively, I expected the Center to have more impressive equipment. Then I remembered that everything must be carried up here by porter or yak.

Back at the Eco Lodge in Lobuche, Henry Todd showed up, larger than life. He has been part of the Himalayan scene for decades. He was the same charming rogue I remembered from Cho Oyu. Henry corrected Victor's story about him running away from authorities for guiding on Denali in Alaska without a permit. In Victor's version, Henry ran into a forest to hide and shivered there all night. In Henry's version, he was in the forest for only a few hours, but he was bitten by many huge mosquitoes that nearly bled him dry.

April 10. As we gained elevation, the quality of the food we ate at lodges worsened. Much of it tasted stale or musty, or it was too greasy. One night I ordered spring rolls, anticipating something with crunchy vegetables inside. Instead, the server brought me grease-soaked rolls filled with over-cooked spaghetti. I could not eat them. At several lodges, the best menu item I found was a fresh tomato and cheese sandwich. I looked forward to Chhongba's cooking at Everest Base Camp. Chhongba was our head cook on Cho Oyu and made some amazing meals there.

Today was Election Day in Nepal. Some of our Sherpas had hiked back to their villages to vote. We heard news about a huge demonstration in San Francisco at the Chinese embassy about the occupation of Tibet. I hoped that unrest would not erupt into violence or cause problems with the Nepalese elections.

Base Camp

A noisy group from Mexico clattered out of the lodge at 4:30 am. No point in trying to go back to sleep, I thought grumpily, crawling out of my sleeping bag. Happily, dawn revealed another bright, clear day, lightening my mood. Sue and I both were recovering from our colds and felt better. As we headed for Everest Base Camp, Mark Sedon and one of our Sherpas set the pace, while Mark Morrison hiked near the back of our group as sweep.

Today hiking felt easy for me, but it challenged others. I could hear Peter and Dave, Phil's police buddies, who were the same age as me, puffing hard behind me. When I was tempted to feel cocky, I reminded myself that we all have good and bad days. Tomorrow I might lag behind them. This is not a race, I reminded myself, trying to quell my competitive impulses.

We hiked to the left of the lower part of the Khumbu Glacier, a river of grimy ice. As desolate as this place looked, the glacier kept reminding us that it was very much alive. Occasionally, we heard an eerie creak or groan from the moving ice. Pack yaks and their handlers, porters carrying loads, other climbers and hikers shambled along among us. Together we resembled a long shimmering necklace of brightly colored beads winding through a vast landscape of brown moraine (rocky debris left by the glacier) and dirty ice.

We arrived at Gorak Shep, the last settlement before Base Camp. Hedd-wyn was here 20 years ago with his wife. Then Gorak Shep was a single stone yak herders' hut, he reminisced happily. Now it had an attractive lodge, where we stopped for noodle soup. There we met Ed Cotter, Guy Cotter's father. At age 81 years, Ed was hiking to Base Camp to visit his Guy. Father and son looked a lot alike. They had the same tall spare figure and craggy good looks – quintessential mountain guys. When we were introduced, Ed bowed, kissed my hand, and wished me well on Everest. I was completely charmed.

After lunch we left Gorak Shep, first trudging through loose sand, then climbing through rocky ridges of moraine. Eventually distant flecks of color grew into dozens of tiny discernable tents, over which towered a distinctive light and dark layered mountain. Lines of ants grew into climbers and hikers crossing the last ridges of moraine to enter Base Camp.

As we approached Base Camp, energy drained from my body like water from a bathtub. Two of our Base Camp Sherpas met us with a kettle of hot Tang. The warm sugary drink gave me a much needed jolt of energy. After a couple of mugs of Tang, someone said, "Let's finish off the bugger," paraphrasing Sir Edmund Hillary's famous announcement to his climbing comrades, after he and Tensing Norgay Sherpa had summited Everest 55 years ago. I felt like part, albeit a very small part, of Everest's grand climbing history, approaching the mountain in Hillary's footsteps.

We picked our way through patches of frozen mud polished slick by others' footsteps, piles of yak dung, boulders balanced on pinnacles of ice, and natural ice caves with icicle fangs. Previous travelers had festooned one of the last ridges with a small forest of elaborate teetering cairns. Past the cairns I started to lose my way among the jumbled rocks and boulders, so I followed the trail of yak dung, as Victor had jokingly advised several days ago.

We passed numerous camps of other expeditions, housing several hundred climbers, guides, and Sherpas. The larger camps included a stone altar topped by a pole radiating strings of colorful prayer flags, forming an "umbrella" of spiritual protection. At last at the far end of Base Camp, I spotted an Adventure Consultants logo on the wall of a long green tent. At its entrance Guy Cotter and Suze Kelly from Adventure Consultants welcomed each of us with a big smile and a handshake. Soft tasteful world music floated surreally from somewhere. This would be our "home" for the next two months.

Our camp was a cluster of tents of different sizes, shapes, and colors pitched in a jumble of ice formations, gray rock, and boulders near the base of the Khumbu Icefall. Huge mountains draped with hanging glaciers surrounded us. The long green tent with the Adventure Consultants logo was our mess tent. Clustered around it were a kitchen tent, guide office tent, Sherpa sleeping tents, medical tent, communication tent, and shower tent. Past the stone altar, behind which loomed the Khumbu Icefall, each guide and client climber had a private sleeping tent, conveniently located near, but not too near, two poo tents and two pee tents.

The Base Camp Sherpas had arrived weeks earlier and claimed Adventure Consultants' usual camp location on the boulder-strewn Khumbu Glacier. The Sherpas had leveled tent sites, pitched tents, and shifted large rock slabs to make walk ways. We had solar panels to charge satellite phones and power a laptop for email and a printer. When there was enough solar power, we could recharge batteries for our cameras and iPods and even watch DVDs. A diesel-fueled generator provided back up power. The Sherpas had furnished the mess tent with a kerosene heater, a long dining table covered with colorful plastic table cloths and decorated with bright plastic flowers. Even the plastic garden chairs were lined with cushions. A portable speaker system broadcasted music from Suze's iPod. These comforts contrasted sharply with the rugged desolate setting.

Our guides gave us a quick briefing about hand washing procedures before entering the mess tent. They emphasized the importance of reducing the risk of gastrointestinal problems, which can spread through camp like wildfire and leave climbers too weak to reach the summit. After we had queued up, washed our hands in soap and warm water from a five-gallon jug, and had used hand sanitizer, we filed into the mess tent for Chhongba's lunch. It was all I had hoped: sushi made with real seaweed and bits of fresh vegetables, miso soup, bagels, New Zealand cheddar cheese, attractively arranged sliced fresh tomatoes and cucumbers, hot ginger tea, and apple pie.

After lunch, Lydia showed me to my sleeping tent between hers and Mike's. Having guides as neighbors was somehow reassuring. Each of our sleeping tents was a generously sized two-person Macpac tent, equipped with plenty of internal mesh pockets for storing gear.

My tent's entrance faced the Khumbu Icefall, a dramatic tumble of giant ice blocks and crevasses 1,800 feet high. I must have done something right in a former life to get this fantastic view! To personalize my tent, I hung five little prayer flags along an outside wall, drew a picture of a trotting fox with Magic Marker, labeled it "SilverFox's Den," and placed it inside a large ZipLoc bag at my tent's entrance. Inside, I unrolled a cheap foam pad next to a thicker sleeping pad provided by Adventure Consultants to make crawling around on my hands and knees more comfortable while unpacking. Buying this cheap pad in Kathmandu was one of Mike's many helpful ideas.

On Cho Oyu, unsure of what I would need, I had brought too much. I had felt overwhelmed by the "tyranny of stuff." The Everest climb would take twice as many weeks as the Cho Oyu climb, but I had brought less this time. Less stuff was easier to organize. I put my ice axe, hiking poles, and crampons just outside the tent and under the rain fly to avoid either ripping the inner tent fabric or losing them. My hat and sunglasses went in the ceiling pocket near the tent entrance, so I would remember to put them on when I went out into the intense high-altitude sun. Clean clothes inside a large compression sack would serve as a pillow. I piled my climbing harness and helmet together, ready for forays into the Khumbu Icefall and beyond. Toiletries, medications, books, reading glasses, and writing materials went into wall pockets where I could reach them easily, when I was in my sleeping bag. Boots and pee bowl stayed in a corner near the tent's entrance. I was determined to be organized and ready on time when we climb, something I did not always achieve on Cho Oyu.

As I unpacked, several avalanches thundered down the nearby peaks. At first I flinched in alarm. Every avalanche sounded like the crack of doom, certain to roar through Base Camp and kill us all. Then my curiosity overcame my fear. I rushed out of my tent to see the spectacle. "Waterfalls" of cascading snow morphed into massive cauliflower clouds of ice crystals. Each avalanche had a mesmerizing, frightening beauty. Daily avalanches became part of our live entertainment in Base Camp.

After sunset, I heard our camp Sherpas call, "Dinner ready," I poked my head outside my sleeping tent. Gently falling snowflakes tickled my face. The guides had warned us about getting chilled, so I dressed for dinner in a down jacket, ski hat, and gloves. Chhongba outdid himself with a fine dinner of Hawaiian pizza, steamed carrots and cauliflower, canned corn and green beans. After dinner, we left the mess tent for our sleeping tents. No one had remembered to bring a headlamp. It was very dark. Outside the mess tent, I became completely disoriented, as though someone had blindfolded me and spun me around. "I'm following Carol," someone said. "Bad idea," I chuckled ruefully as I stumbled into something, probably a boulder, and then slid on a patch of unseen ice.

After eventually finding my sleeping tent, I did not sleep much. Avalanches thundered down the mountains surrounding Base Camp throughout the night. Each one jolted me awake from an uneasy half sleep. The glacier cracked, moaned, and shifted under my tent like a restless beast. Occasionally icebergs calved and crashed into a frozen lake behind my tent. I was excited to finally be at Base Camp and about to begin our climb. I also was a little scared.

Puja and Practice

April 11. By 5:30 am, it was getting light, and I had had enough "tent time." I put on hiking boots, ski hat, jacket, and gloves, and took a walk around camp. Everest Base Camp was cleaner than I expected, a pleasant surprise. Yak dung was everywhere, but there was little trash or human waste. Our poo tents were built over barrels lined with plastic bags, so all solid human waste could be sealed and hauled off the mountain.

As the sky lightened, I could see Sherpas wreathing Guy Cotter in katas and shaking hands with him. He was preparing to hike back to Lukla. I went over to say goodbye. I felt a little sad, as I watched him go. Restless, I continued my stroll around our cluster of tents. Kami and Sanghe, two of our Base Camp Sherpas, intercepted me with a steaming face cloth, hot tea, smiles, and namastes.

Others were stirring now. As they emerged from their sleeping tents, we exchanged good mornings and compared notes about our first night in Base Camp. Mark Cohen, Cheryl and Nikki's media guy, moaned in comic self-mockery, "Nothing worked. The sleeping bag didn't work, the mattress didn't work, the socks didn't work..." Apparently he had slid off his air mattress and had gotten chilled from sleeping on the icy floor of his tent.

Chhongba made a lavish breakfast of scrambled eggs and bacon, porridge, a choice of cold cereals, canned fruit, pancakes with real 100% Canadian maple syrup, yogurt made from reconstituted powdered milk and starter culture, milk tea, black tea, and coffee. As good as breakfast was, we did not linger over it. A lama would perform a puja today in our camp. The purpose of the puja, as I understood it, was to ask the local mountain deities for forgiveness for poking Everest with our crampons and to request safety during our climb. We scattered to our sleeping tents to get crampons, axes, mountaineering boots, and harnesses to be blessed at the puja altar.

A young lama, resplendent in a red fedora, sat on an improvised cushion in front of the puja altar, and chanted prayers. An assistant used a curved drum stick to tap a gentle rhythm on a wide shallow drum decorated with painted dragons. Unlike traditional Western church services during which everyone sits quietly, guides and climbers got up, strolled around, and found better angles to photograph the puja. Some Sherpas talked and joked among themselves. Devout Sherpas who knew the prayers chanted them along with the lama. Others fed springs of juniper into a small smoky fire on the altar. We each took a generous pinch from a place of raw rice and, when Ang Dorje signaled us, we tossed it three times toward the altar, murmuring "so, so, so." During breaks in the ceremony, the young lama sipped tea, chatted, and laughed with the Sherpas.

At the end of the ceremony, the mood turned playful. A plate of tsampa (roasted barley flour) was passed around. We grabbed handfuls of it, rubbed it on each other's faces and tossed it into the air. The flour on our faces represented hope that we would live long lives and grow white beards. Beer, chang, and whiskey flowed freely, along with conversation and laughter. Henry Todd showed up and joined in the fun. Choughs, miniature ravens with yellow beaks and red feet, took a break from playing in the thermals and swooped down to snatch crumbs from cookies and Pringles. They flew so close I could hear the swish of their wings.

The mood became solemn, as we made amulets from Lama Geshe's folded prayer bundles and golden threads. The amulets had to be covered in white, so Ang Dorje and Ang Tsering helped us wrap them in white athletic tape. Lama Geshe had instructed us to wear these amulets at all times near our hearts, until we completed our climb. I carefully put my amulet on and settled it under my layers of clothing. It might not help, but it would not hurt.

Protected now according to Sherpa custom, Cheryl invited me to join her and Nikki for a short walk back through Base Camp toward Lobuche. Our guides had recommended light activity to help us acclimatize, so the walk seemed like a good idea. I joined Cheryl and Nikki, grateful for this kind offer. I had been concerned about being the odd woman out.

After our walk, we met in the mess tent for a briefing from the guides about the next six weeks. The guides explained that we would make several forays up and down the mountain to help us acclimatize, using the "climb high, sleep low" method. For our first acclimatization cycle, we would climb part way through the Khumbu Icefall and return to Base Camp to sleep. After a day or two of rest, we would climb further into the Icefall and return to Base Camp. The next climb, we would go to Camp 1 at 19,600 feet elevation and sleep there, returning to Base Camp the next morning. We would complete at least two additional acclimatization cycles, spending nights at Camp 2 at 20,800 feet elevation and Camp 3 at 23,500 feet elevation. Before the final climb to the summit, we would descend to the relatively thick air of Pheriche to rest and fatten up. That was the plan, but military restrictions, weather, and the condition of the climbing route could change everything.

Back in my sleeping tent, I read Dai Sijie's "Balzac and the Little Chinese Seamstress," which Lydia had finished and loaned me. It is the story of three Chinese teenagers during the Cultural Revolution and reminded me of my former boss, Wu. As I settled into reading, afternoon snow pattered against my tent's walls, making a peaceful soothing sound. A large avalanche thundered down. I scrambled out of my tent to watch it. Our hikers and their guides, the two Marks, were leaving Base Camp for Island Peak. I put on a hat and jacket and went over to them to say goodbye. I would miss them.

April 12. After breakfast, Mike introduced me to Tendi Sherpa. He was about my height, but stockier and heavier than me. He greeted me with a broad, agreeable smile as we shook hands. Tendi would be my climbing partner above Base Camp. He would stay with me in case I was slower than the rest of the team.

The guides helped us rig our ascender and safety, each on its own leash attached to our climbing harness. An ascender is a metal device that clips onto a fixed line, a rope fixed to a mountain slope to protect climbers if they fall. When using an ascender, a climber takes a couple of steps up the slope and then slides the ascender up the fixed line, where it catches and holds through a ratchet mechanism, keeping the climber attached to the fixed line and creating a mechanical hand hold on the fixed line. The climber then climbs up a couple more steps and slides the ascender up the fixed line again.

The safety is a carabiner, an oval metal loop with a spring gate, which the climber clips onto the fixed line just ahead of the ascender. Unlike the ascender, the safety runs freely on the rope. Each time the climber comes to a piece of protection (a point at which the fixed line is attached to the mountain,) the climber must remove the safety and reclip it onto the fixed line past the piece of protection, followed by the ascender. If done correctly, the climber is always attached to the fixed line by the ascender, the safety, or both.

With my ascender and safety rigged to my climbing harness, I stumbled through the boulders, rock, and ice in my bulky mountaineering boots to the foot of the Khumbu Icefall. The Sherpas had prepared a training course for us to practice skills we would need in the Khumbu Icefall. I was nervous. As I gazed up a steep ice wall, one of the Sherpas was front pointing (climbing with only his crampon's forward points jabbed into the steep ice) up a fixed line. Suddenly his line ripped loose, and the Sherpa sailed

Hedd-wyn Williams, Carol Masheter, and Tendi Sherpa at Everest Base Camp, harnesses rigged for climbing in the Khumbu Icefall, April 12, 2008, photo by Lydia Bradey.

outward from the wall. My scalp jumped in horror. The Sherpa, still attached to the fixed line, giggled and bounced back onto the wall, then resumed his climb. Would that happen to me, I wondered. I swallowed anxiously. My throat was very dry.

Near the base of the ice wall, we put on crampons. Tendi and I checked each other's levers and straps for proper placement and tightness. Mark was setting up to film Cheryl and Nikki. Simon wanted to borrow crampons, so he could try the course. Excitement swept through our group.

Our first challenge was to walk across a ladder bridge about 18 inches above the ground. The bridge was two aluminum ladders tied together, the end of the first overlapping the end of the second by about two feet. Everyone else did really well. Then it was my turn. I had practiced with an old aluminum ladder back home, but this looked harder. My breath came in anxious little gasps. I tried to convince myself that even if I fell off this low practice bridge, I could not get hurt.

I clipped a safety to each of the two waist-high hand ropes, one on its own leash, the other clipped to my ascender. I bridged two ladder rungs with a bulky cramponed boot and transferred my weight to it. I bridged the next two rungs with the other boot, and weighted it. Now my trailing boot's crampons were stuck in the ladder's rungs. "Take a step back to free it," Mike advised. I picked up my front foot, felt behind myself for stable footing, and shifted my weight onto it. Now my other foot was stuck. Great, I thought wryly, I am walking backwards. Maybe I should turn around and cross the ladder bridge backwards. I leaned backwards and wiggled the stuck crampon free. "Step so your arch is over only one rung," Mike suggested. I tried that, but I wobbled too much and felt like I would fall off the ladder bridge. I tried stepping on the sides of the ladder, but Mike warned, "The ladder will flip sideways, if you do that." I returned to bridging two rungs with each boot, trying to position the crampon teeth so they would not get stuck. I inched across the practice bridge at a snail's pace. I crossed it a couple more times, getting stuck less often and gaining confidence.

We moved onto other challenges. We climbed the steep ice wall, from which the Sherpa had taken his dramatic swing. At the top of this wall, we climbed a narrow undulating ridge of ice, traversed it, and crossed a couple more ladder bridges spanning deeper drops than the practice bridge. Then we transferred from fixed lines to ladders on steep slopes and rappelled, a technique of walking down a steep face while using friction on a rope to control the speed of descent. I tripped and fell during a tricky traversing rappel. Stupid! Clumsy! shrieked my inner critic. Shut up, I growled back at my critic. "Do it again," ordered Mike. I got up and got it right the second time. Tendi cheered. Mike grinned.

Practice had gone better than I had expected. My confidence returned. "I can do this!" my inner optimist crowed.

84

Lower Lake Land

April 13. I woke up surrounded by sparkling ice crystals. Frozen moisture from my breath lined the inside of my tent. Today we would climb in the actual Icefall about one quarter of the way, cross the first few ladders, and then return to Base Camp.

After breakfast, Mike took Tendi and me aside. "Carol, you set the pace, so Super Sherpa Tendi here does not go too fast," he instructed. "Come on, grandma," Tendi teased as he turned to leave for the Icefall. I bristled. Maybe I was being overly sensitive about my age, but Tendi's teasing bugged me. I replied bluntly, "Don't call me that. You may call me Carol Didi (older sister)." From that moment, he called me Carol Didi, and I called him Tendi Bai (younger brother).

At the puja altar we each took a pinch of rice and tossed it three times, then passed the altar on our right. Following Tendi's surefooted steps toward the Icefall, I slipped and slid clumsily down talus (loose rock on a slope) on top of ice, trying not to fall and look like an idiot. We picked our way through boulders along a partially frozen stream of glacial melt. A shaggy lump materialized into a yak, resting on the ice. It stared at us dully and did not get up. Past the yak, we put on our crampons and checked each other's bindings and climbing harness. It was time to climb.

We picked our way through Lower Lake Land, Victor's whimsical name for the lower part of the Icefall. Lower Lake Land was about two dozen giant frozen ripples in the glacier. We climbed up each ripple, some of which were at least 30 feet high, then climbed down its other side. I noticed I was hauling myself up the fixed lines, using my arms too much, tiring myself more than necessary. I focused on good placement of my feet on little ledges and less steep places on the ice and using the big muscles in my legs. I tried to imitate Tendi, who seemed to climb effortlessly and without slipping or falling.

Between the giant ripples were narrow frozen lakes. While skirting one of the lakes, my left boot broke through the ice and I sank nearly to my knee in icy water. Thanks to the integrated design of my mountaineering boots, my foot stayed dry, a lucky break. Beyond Lower Lake Land, the climbing became steeper. It was far from being the most difficult ice climbing I had done, but at 18,000 feet elevation it was very hard work.

I climbed slowly, as Mike suggested. Others passed Tendi and me, triggering my competitive impulses. I had gotten used to being near the front of the group during our hike to Base Camp. I was tempted to speed up, so I could keep up with the rest of the team. I reminded myself, slow is good. Don't get discouraged about being last. Just keep going.

We scrambled through a chaotic jumble of giant blocks of ice, some as big as houses. Weird ice formations loomed over us like monsters. We did not pause near anything overhanging, because of the danger of falling ice. At last, we crossed a short ladder bridge, then three more.

If I let my gaze travel down into the seemingly bottomless crevasses, I felt a mixture of fear and awe – fear of falling into them and awe at their beautiful turquoise depths. I forced myself to focus only on where to place my feet on the ladder. My ladder crossing was slow and cautious yet sound.

I was pleased to have crossed real ladder bridges rather than the practice bridges, but I was exhausted. I wondered how on earth I would climb through the entire Icefall, never mind higher on the mountain. Mercifully, the guides said it was time to return to Base Camp. Going back down was easier on my heart and lungs but trickier for my feet. Right in front of a group of handsome young guys moving up the Icefall, I caught a crampon, tripped, and fell, sprawling at their feet. "Are you OK?" one asked, in a tone of polite concern. "Only my dignity is hurt," I replied, trying to cover my embarrassment with humor.

After we returned from our first foray into the Icefall, our guides attended a meeting with a military liaison officer. The officer told them that no one would be allowed to climb in the Icefall tomorrow. Apparently the Chinese were concerned that protestors might interfere with the Olympic Torch relay. I wondered irritably what the Chinese thought climbers could do at this high elevation that could be disruptive.

Like it or not, we were subject to the restrictions, backed up by armed guards. Our plan for tomorrow had been to climb half way through the Icefall. Since that no longer was an option, we would hike back toward Gorak Shep and climb Kala Patar, a peak of 18,000 feet elevation, to encourage our bodies to acclimatize.

Since we had arrived in Base Camp, I had been experiencing periodic breathing at night. Just as I was about to fall asleep, I would take a deep breath, which would jerk me awake. I was not getting enough sleep.

I asked Mike and Simon for advice. They both suggested taking Diamox at night. I had had a negative reaction to sulfa drugs a few years ago, when I was being treated for antibiotic resistant pneumonia. Doctors had been reluctant to prescribe Diamox for me, because it is related to sulfa drugs, so I had not used Diamox before.

Weeks of poor sleep had been a problem for me on Cho Oyu. I was willing to try Diamox with a physician nearby in case of another negative reaction. Taking about 60 milligrams of Diamox (a quarter of a pill) at night evened out my breathing and did not cause any problems, other than the usual side effect of increased urination.

Between needing to pee every two hours and several loud avalanches, I still did not sleep much, but I felt more rested.

Kala Patar

April 14. The rising sun revealed a clear blue sky, a good day to climb Kala Patar. After breakfast, we each went to the storage area in the rear of the mess tent and chose food for today's climb. The storage area included a wide array of snacks from three continents -- cookies, candy bars, crackers, nuts, dried fruit, and Pringles to name a few. Back home, I did not buy these goodies, because they were too tempting, and I tended to over indulge. On Everest, where I was working hard in cold air with less than half the oxygen at sea level, I needed plenty of calories and could eat anything, including these "forbidden" foods. Ironically, none of them looked very appealing.

I loaded my pack with extra warm clothes, two liters of water, a chapatti rolled up with boysenberry jam and peanut butter, roasted almonds, dried fruit, jelly beans, and a Snickers bar. I hoped I would be able to eat at least some of these goodies during our climb. Tendi offered to carry my pack again. He added his one liter water bottle and a package of cookies then shouldered my pack. His minimalism was impressive. Cheryl teased me about the attention I got from Tendi and threatened to steal him. I snarled at her in mock fierceness. Tendi smiled shyly.

We snaked through Base Camp around clusters of tents belonging to other expeditions and over mounds of rock and ice toward Kala

Patar. Distant chanting and drumming floated from other camps having their puja today. We crossed a dip in the moraine and climbed up onto the well traveled ridge that led to Base Camp. Along the way, where climbers turn off to approach the peak, Pumori, we paused and looked back. We were rewarded by a fine view of Everest's summit with its characteristic banner cloud of wind-driven spindrift, a wall of blowing snow that extended from the summit. When the village of Gorak Shep came into view, we left the ridge and traversed up the dry rocky slope with the glacier on our left, taking a more direct cross country route to Kala Patar through talus (loose rock on a slope) and patches of scrawny brown vegetation, still dormant and waiting for spring.

As Tendi and I climbed over boulders the last hundred yards to the summit, a cold storm raced up the valley. The view of Everest disappeared behind a curtain of fast-moving clouds. Pellets of wind-driven snow stung my face. Cold crept through my layers of clothing like the blunt noses of insistent hounds. Near the summit, I huddled behind a cluster of boulders to put on more clothes. The wind snatched and twisted my climbing bibs, as I struggled to put them on.

Tendi joyfully pulled a string of prayer flags from his jacket. He scampered over the last few boulders and added his flags to the flapping mass already on the summit. Tendi rejoined me in the lee of the boulders, grinning broadly and looking very pleased. "First summit of Kala Patar," he said. I ate a handful of almonds and drank water, then stood and faced the gusting wind. I staggered down the barren rocky mountain, as the wind blew me off balance. While we descended, Lydia took a picture of Tendi and me, grinning happily, pleased with our summit.

We were back in Base Camp four hours after we had set off that morning. Back home, this would have been a short easy hike, with plenty of time afterwards to buy the week's groceries and mow the lawn. Here, climbing at 18,000 feet elevation in strong wind had left me tired, cold, and hungry. I ducked into the mess tent and finished the snacks I had carried up the mountain. I drank as much water as I could, remembering that proper hydration helps acclimatization. I noticed Tendi's unopened package of cookies in my pack. I found his tent and returned them. "For next time," I grinned. He grinned back. I felt good about our budding partnership.

The storm left Base Camp as suddenly as it had assaulted us on Kala Patar. I crawled into my sun-warmed sleeping tent to read. The trapped heat felt wonderful after getting chilled during the brief storm. The sudden change in weather reminded me never to be complacent in the mountains.

One aspect of high altitude mountaineering that books and documentaries often omit is the alternation between periods of extreme effort and extreme laziness. To acclimatize, climbers need to stress their bodies enough to trigger adaptive changes, such as growing more red blood cells and changing the pH of the blood. The body requires rest to make these changes. Finding the right balance between stress and rest is not easy. Too much stress breaks down the body. Too much rest does not sufficiently acclimatize the body. During previous climbs of big mountains, I had seen ashen-faced climbers, who could not find this balance, staggering down the mountain after a failed summit attempt. I wanted to do everything I could to avoid that unhappy fate.

After our climb up Kala Patar, several of us gathered in the mess tent. I enjoyed comparing both mother-daughter teams' experiences on Kilimanjaro and Aconcagua with mine. I listened eagerly as they described their experiences on mountains I had not yet climbed. North Face was sponsoring Cheryl and Nikki and had provided them with mountaineering clothing, sleeping bags, and other gear. I especially envied their warm, sturdy camp boots. My own flimsy down booties helped keep my feet warm in my sleeping bag, but they were not substantial enough to wear around camp. Roxi told us proudly about Robyn's world class status as a mountain bike racer, while Robyn quietly blushed.

Popcorn

April 16. I awoke at 4:30 am to the hiss of stoves in the kitchen tent and the scent of burning juniper from the puja altar. Our Sherpas burned juniper on days when we climbed above Base Camp. Today the military would let us climb half way through the Icefall. It was time to get up.

I felt a sense of cold dread. Two days ago I had been exhausted after climbing only one quarter of the way. How would I climb twice as far into the higher more challenging parts of the Icefall? I told my doubts to shut up. Think about what you need to do in the next five minutes, then in the next hour, I reminded myself. You can do this.

The temperature was18 degrees Fahrenheit when I left my sleeping tent. Later in the day, when the sun would be high in the sky, the Icefall could become a giant reflector oven. I dressed in layers: sweat-wicking bra and briefs, base layer top and bottoms, wind jacket, glacier pants, buff (a tube of synthetic cloth that can serve as a neck gaiter, face mask, or hat), ski hat, sweat-wicking liner socks under thicker wool socks, climbing harness with ascender and safety, mountaineering boots. I would be able to regulate my body temperature by removing layers from my upper body, if I got too hot.

I went to the mess tent for breakfast, a more Spartan meal of cereal, canned fruit, and toast than Chhongba's extravagant rest-day breakfasts. I shoveled food into a stomach still not quite awake. Then I went to the storage area and stared dully at shelves of snacks, trying to decide what I could eat up there.

As we climbed through Lower Lake Lands, the sky lightened. Pumori, rising behind us, blazed with alpine glow -- first bronze, then peach, then pale gold. The seracs and crevasses turned from gray to translucent turquoise. Some leaning seracs wore sparkling garlands of icicles. I felt a sense of wonder, as though I were exploring an alien planet. I wanted to stop and photograph, but we were climbing in one of the less stable parts of the Icefall. Stopping would increase the risk of getting squashed by a falling serac.

Above the four ladder bridges we crossed last time, the route became steeper. The ladder bridges were longer and more wobbly. As I approached each bridge, I took deep slow breaths and focused on what I needed to do. Focusing on these simple but essential tasks was a challenge. My fear of heights rose like molten lava from my gut to my throat each time I approached another bridge. My eyes were tempted to look down into the terrifying depths of the crevasse the bridge spanned. Because the body often follows the gaze, I knew if I looked down, I was more likely to fall down. I focused on looking only where I needed to place my feet.

On some of the longer steeper pitches of ice I had to pause to catch my breath. One by one, my team mates and the guides passed Tendi and me. Gray-faced, Hedd-wyn complained, "I feel like shit." As Steve sped past Hedd-wyn, Tendi, and me, he said over his shoulder, "You guys are my heroes." I stared at him dully, panting to get enough air. I did not feel very heroic at the moment.

An hour later Tendi and I caught up to the rest of our team during a rest stop. We took rest stops away from overhanging seracs. What a relief it was to stop, even for a few minutes. We followed our usual ritual of self-care tasks: take off our pack, place it so it would not slide down the mountain, sit down, drink water, eat a snack, take a pee, put on sun screen, clean eye wear, take off or put on layers of clothing. If I could not finish all of these tasks during one rest stop, I would start where I left off at the next stop.

As I was eating a handful of "fox food," my own mixture of dried fruit, nuts and M & Ms, Victor's ice axe got loose and slid down the ice toward me. I grabbed the sliding axe and teased, "Thought this was a safe zone, Victor," and jammed my climbing helmet onto my head as a joke. Mike cackled and said Victor owed each of us pina colatas. We howled with laughter. Mountaineer humor. Maybe you had to have been there to "get it."

We crossed about 15 ladder bridges in the Popcorn, a particularly complex jumble of teetering seracs, ice boulders, and deep crevasses. The last ladder we climbed today was four ladders lashed together up a steep ice wall. Though this wall ladder creaked and wobbled as much as the ladder bridges, I found it less scary. It was easier to avoid looking down, while I climbed up a wall ladder. At the top of the ladder, I transitioned to a fixed line on a steep wall, and then climbed up onto an uneven shelf. There, others were resting and snacking. We were at nearly 19,000 feet elevation, higher than planned. The guides were pleased.

Nikki, Cheryl, and I moved away from the group for a communal pee, standing in a line and using our pee funnels. Though easier and safer than having to loosen our harnesses, lower our pants, and squat, getting the funnels lined up correctly through climbing harness, ascender and safety leashes, zippers, and layers of clothing was no simple task. Someone from another expedition was filming behind us. "We could be immortalized in someone's documentary. At least our backs are to the camera," I joked. We giggled companionably at this absurd situation, as we zipped our flies and returned to where the others were resting. More mountaineer humor.

More climbers from other expeditions stopped to rest near us. An attractive young guy, feeling generous after his climb into the Icefall, offered me a cookie. Another young man named Rob remembered me from Aconcagua. I basked in the camaraderie of mountaineers, sharing simple pleasures of rest, cookies, and memories of other climbs. For so much of my life I had felt like the shy nerdy outsider. Today I relished this sense of belonging.

After our brief rest stop, we headed back down to Base Camp. I have often found climbing down scarier than climbing up. To climb down, I must look down, riling up my fear-of-heights demons. Today I focused on my feet, looking for little flat areas, bumps, or edges I could leverage into foot holds and planted as many crampon points as possible into the ice. This preoccupation with my feet kept me from looking too far down and helped keep my fear manageable. Tendi and I passed some of our team mates. Lydia praised my footwork. My confidence rose. Piece of cake, this mountain, my inner optimist crowed. Here you were all scared, and Lydia, a world-class mountaineer, is complimenting your footwork.

At the training course where we practiced a few days ago, Simon and Laurel met us with a teapot of cold instant mango drink and Cokes. I was surprised how thirsty I was. The mango drink tasted wonderful. Fueled by sugar, I scrambled through boulders and ice for another 15 minutes to Base Camp, just after Mike, Hedd-wyn, and Phil.

After the sugar rush, I was bone tired. However, I was no more exhausted than when we climbed only half as far through the Icefall two days ago. My body seemed to be acclimatizing. I felt encouraged. Satisfied with the day's labors, I enjoyed Chhongba's delicious Sherpa pie, a mixture of hardy vegetables topped by mashed potatoes and cheese, followed by a slice of dense banana cake.

Climbers descending part of the Khumbu Icefall, April 16, 2008, photo by Mike Roberts.

Hear No Evil, Speak No Evil

A communication black out has been announced. Our military liaison officer has ordered us to turn over all email devices, satellite telephones, and video cameras. The military would confiscate any equipment we did not voluntarily surrender. They would conduct unannounced searches of our tents. After my initial shock and indignation, I worried the sudden black out would alarm friends and family back home. I also worried that our confiscated equipment would not be returned.

We were allowed to phone and email one last time before the black out began. We were not to mention the black out or use words like email, satellite phone, communication, or video camera, as the guides suspected the military was eavesdropping on our calls and emails. We were told not to even say these words around camp, because Sherpa spies could overhear and report us. So we used code words and hand signals: "tin can" for satellite phone, waggling fingers over an imaginary keyboard for email, and a bent elbow with the hand retracted inside an empty sleeve for a video camera. I emailed my friends and sister and tried to reassure them that all was well, even if they did not hear from me for awhile.

Our guides turned over our email laptops and phones except one of our satellite phones, which they hid. They would use it to send brief secret messages to the Adventure Consultants office in New Zealand, which the staff would post as dispatches on the Adventure Consultants web site. That way, our friends and family would have at least some news during the black out.

Some of us found ways to defy the unannounced tent searches. One of the guys left a dirty magazine open just inside his tent, hoping it would repel the military inspector. Instead the inspector told him to give him the magazine. Nice try. Some of us women buried our contraband among our unmentionables. That seemed to work better than the dirty magazine.

Rumors buzzed through Base Camp about a climber the military had forced to leave the mountain. Apparently he had shown a banner protesting the Chinese occupation of Tibet. The military found out about it and summarily compelled him to leave. To those of us accustomed to free expression, this incident was a harsh reminder that people in other parts of the world do not follow our rules. Our best hope was that the Olympic Torch relay team would summit soon, so the restrictions would lift, and we could finally climb this mountain.

April 18. Today would be a rest day, at least for our guides and team members. Our 18 climbing Sherpas would climb through the Icefall and establish Camp 1 at 19,600 feet. At 5 am, I heard murmured prayers, as Sherpas passed the puja altar. They returned before noon, while I was finishing my hand laundry. They had carried heavy loads through the entire Icefall in the time it took us to climb halfway. We all stood, applauded, and cheered. The Sherpas grinned shyly, as they filed past with empty packs and the easy stride of wiry men bred and born in the Himalayas. What would we do without these guys?

Today each climber would see Simon for a base-line physical. When it was my turn, Simon checked my heart rate, oxygen saturation, and my lungs. He said everything seemed fine. He gave me preventive asthma medication to inhale twice a day, which he has been encouraging other team members to use. I was wary of any new medication, but I was relieved to have "passed muster." I dutifully started using the asthma medication.

Mike has gone to another meeting with the military. At dinner some team members grumbled about his frequent absences and general unavailability. About midway through dinner, he joined us with news. The military would not permit anyone to climb through the Icefall to Camp 1 tomorrow.

Discouraged, I wondered whether we would ever be allowed to climb this mountain. Some years ago, an acquaintance of mine paid for a permit to climb Everest from the Tibet side. At the last minute he was denied permission to climb. He was not reimbursed for his permit, and he never got another chance at Everest. This seemed to be happening to us, too. I thought angrily this could be the most expensive hike to Base Camp on record. In my sleeping tent, I fought bitter tears of frustration – and lost. I cried like a baby.

April 19. Since we were not allowed to climb to Camp 1 today, Victor offered to lead an acclimatization hike to Pumori Base Camp. We took the now very familiar walk back through Everest Base Camp, crossed the dip in the moraine to the well worn ridge trail, picked our way down into a large trough, and then climbed up a steep boulder-strewn ridge. We found traces of a camp overlooking a partially frozen lake, milky blue with glacial silt. As we rested behind boulders out of the wind, we admired a fine view of Everest. Today tendrils of spindrift swirled around its dark summit like soft wispy hair, a bit like Hedd-wyn's. We returned to Everest Base Camp in time for Chhongba's excellent Sherpa soup of potatoes, cauliflower, and carrots.

Today was Passover. Cheryl supervised the preparation of Passover foods in the cook tent. At dinner in the mess tent Nikki and Mark Cohen chanted prayers in Hebrew. They patiently explained the verses and the symbolic foods we passed around the table. Crisp thin papadam stood in for the unleavened bread the Hebrew slaves took during their flight from Egypt. Hard boiled eggs symbolized new life. Grated apples and walnuts represented the mortar the slaves used to build the pyramids. Bitter herbs signified their sorrow and suffering. I appreciated our Jewish team members' willingness to include us in their beloved tradition. Afterwards, we went to bed early. The military would permit us to climb to Camp 1 tomorrow.

The Valley of Silence

April 20. At 3:30 am, I pulled on layers of clothing, getting ready to climb. After a quick breakfast, we tossed rice at the puja altar and left camp at 4:30 am. We climbed to the first ladders in about 90 minutes, a personal best for me. I puffed hard climbing up the giant ice ridges, but my breathing was steady and strong. Mike teasingly called me a "steam engine."

Some of the ladder bridges above where we last climbed were very scary. One near the top of the Icefall consisted of five ladders lashed together to span a huge seemingly bottomless crevasse. It looked like the Ladder Bridge from Hell. We joined a long queue of climbers and Sherpas with loads waiting to cross it. Only one climber could cross at a time. One guy from another expedition was so unnerved he crossed it on his hands and knees. I could always do that if I had to. I licked my very dry lips.

It was my turn. Panic rose in my gut like a witch's brew. Focus and do what you know how to do, I reminded myself. You can do this. Breathe. The ladder bounced up and down, swayed side to side, and tried to twist and dump me into the crevasse. By the time I had inched half way across, the bridge seemed to move in at least 17 dimensions. I froze, my knees shaking like Jell-o. I felt like I was going to vomit. I murmured, "Om mani padme hoom" (a

Buddhist prayer that means roughly, "hail to the jewel in the heart of the lotus.") Don't look down into the crevasse. Look where to put one foot on the ladder, then the other. One of my crampons got stuck in the ladder's rungs. I shifted my weight backwards and freed it. I chanted, "Om mani padme hoom, take a step, om mani padme hoom," took another a step. Almost there. Don't get complacent. Stay focused. Finally my crampons bit ice instead of metal. I was drenched in nervous sweat, but I was across the Ladder Bridge From Hell.

It was not over. We had several more ladders to cross or climb. One steep wall required five ladders roped together and propped against it to get up most of the way, then climbers transferred from the ladder to steep ice using a fixed line, made a dicey traverse on a narrow ledge, and climbed another ladder. The ladders bounced and swayed away from the wall as we climbed. Some sections were so steep I had to lean backwards to see where to place my feet. After the Ladder Bridge from Hell, however, my jitters were gone. Perhaps I was too tired to waste energy on being afraid.

After we climbed the last wall ladder, we took a rest break at the top of the Icefall. Mike called me "flying fox" because of my faster pace today. I was as pleased as an attention-hungry child with his praise.

We had climbed the Icefall in shadow. Now the late morning sun was turning our rest place into a giant oven. The sunlight reflected from the glacier was so intense, it hurt my eyes. We shed layers of clothing, applied lots of sunscreen, and put on glacier goggles.

We were at the entrance of the Western Cwm (pronounced "koom"), also known as the Valley of Silence, a long vast valley of white glacial ice and snow flanked by huge mountains. At first, the route to Camp 1 looked easy compared to climbing through the Icefall. However, as we continued, we could see several huge crevasses too wide for ladder bridges. We had to climb down into each crevasse, weave our way through giant blocks of ice that formed an uneasy bottom, then climb out the other side. These big crevasses caused

A climber nearing the top of the Khumbu Icefall, April 20, 2008, photo by Carol Masheter.

traffic jams, because the steep descents and ascents using fixed lines were slow, with few places for faster climbers to pass slower ones.

At last, tiny tents appeared in the distance. As happy as I was to see Camp 1, fatigue from today's climb hit me like a ton of bricks. My body felt like lead here at 19,500 feet elevation. Tendi strolled effortlessly ahead of me, while I dragged myself up and down the last few giant ripples in the glacier to our tents. It seemed to take forever. At our tents at last, I tried to conceal my fatigue from the others, as well as myself, with my happy SilverFox howl, "AAAHHHOOOO!!!"

I stripped off my crampons and organized my gear inside my tent. I unpacked my sleeping pad, sleeping bag, mug, bowl, and spoon. Our toilet at Camp 1 was a narrow designated crevasse behind a low snow wall about 50 yards from our tents. Meals were far simpler here than Chhongba's elaborate spreads. Zangbu brought me a chapatti with a sealed packet of warmed tomato sauce. My Swiss army knife was down in Base Camp, so I stabbed the tough plastic sauce packet with a crampon to open it. Then Zangbu brought reconstituted powdered mushroom soup, white rice, and tea.

Victor stopped by and asked whether I would be warm enough sleeping alone, as everyone else was sharing tents. I know what you're thinking. No, Victor was not giving me a come on. At least I did not think so. However, I am hopelessly clueless about these matters, so who knows? I assured him with a sly grin that I would be fine on my own in my minus 40 degree down sleeping bag.

April 21. At 10 am, we left Camp 1 for an acclimatization climb, planning to go about half way to Camp 2. Soon we were climbing down into a giant crevasse and up the other side. We repeated the process with a second and a third crevasse. At nearly 20,000 feet elevation, the steep climbing into and out of crevasses was strenuous. My legs felt dull and heavy. Robyn said she felt sick. Hedd-wyn and Steve were slower than usual and seemed tired. Phil and the guides were feeling strong today. I reminded myself that we all have good days and bad days at high altitude. As long as the bad days did not outnumber the good ones, I coached myself.

As we climbed, our guides complained that this route was not the usual way to Camp 2. After we had climbed through the third deep crevasse, the guides decided this route was not safe. We headed back toward Camp 1. I said a little prayer of thanks. I was not sure I could have climbed much higher today – and we still had to climb back through the three big crevasses. At least we met today's goal of four hours of acclimatization activity.

Boulders of ice and snow strewn through our camp indicated we were in an avalanche path. We decided to move our tents to a safer location. I worked with Tendi to chop and level new tent sites with our ice axes on the next ice ridge. I appreciated all the hard work the Sherpas did, so we would have a better chance to reach the summit. I felt more like a "real" mountaineer, when I helped the Sherpas with some of the camp duties.

As we worked, rumors drifted through Camp 1 like poisonous gas. Some climbers with other expeditions reported that the military was deliberately delaying the Icefall doctors' progress in putting in ladder bridges and fixed lines above us to Camp 2. The Icefall doctors were Sherpas who specialized in establishing the route through the Ice Fall. Others complained that the military had said we could move up the mountain then changed their minds the next day. "Broken agreements," they growled, "We're screwed if we play their game, and we're screwed if we don't." The rumors were unsettling, a reminder that the military could end our climb at any time.

Home Away From Home

April 22. At 6 am it was 25 degrees Fahrenheit, sunny and calm, good weather to head down to Base Camp. I finished separating clothing and gear that would stay at Camp 1 from what I would carry down to Base Camp. Tendi and I left at 7:45 am. The Icefall doctors had put double ladders across some of the broader crevasses and up some of the higher ice walls, which eased some of the traffic jams. We rappelled down some of the walls instead of using the crowded ladders. I found rappelling here clumsy, which I attributed to the lower level of oxygen, less than half of the oxygen back home. I faced my nemesis, the Ladder Bridge From Hell, and crossed it without incident, a triumph for me.

There was a lot of traffic in the Icefall today. We passed several climbers, their eyes dull with fatigue, also coming down from higher on the mountain. Others were moving up to Camp 1. Tendi seemed to know all the Sherpas. They exchanged greetings and jokes in their own language. "Namaste" was the extent of my contribution.

We crossed the last ladder bridge and entered Lower Lake Lands. Climbing up and down the two dozen giant ridges of ice was easy compared to higher in the Icefall, but after hours of climbing, my body felt like a car running out of gasoline and coasting on fumes. At last, as I tramped along the stream of snow melt from the Icefall, I was relieved to see Laurel standing above us on the ridge of moraine near our puja altar in Base Camp. I howled my happy SilverFox howl, "AAAHHHOOOO!!!" She howled back. I laughed out loud, delighted with her imitation.

Ah, Base Camp. When we first arrived, it had seemed bleak and alien, a tangle of gray boulders, rock, and dirty ice. By now it had become a cozy cluster of tents with many exotic comforts -- showers, clean clothes, more varied and tastier food, thicker air, bigger appetites, and better sleep. Miraculously, Base Camp had become home. It felt wonderful to be here.

I went to my sleeping tent and dropped off my pack and climbing gear, exchanged my mountaineering boots for old running shoes, and joined the others in the mess tent. Chhongba's sushi, sliced fresh Asian pears, tomatoes, and cucumbers tasted especially good. Laurel, Simon, and Mark, the Barts' media guy, seemed genuinely happy to see us. Camp was too quiet without us, they said. Laurel gave me an encouraging message from Jan Orton, someone I knew from work, who had figured out how to get past the communication blackout. Jan's persistence and ingenuity touched me; I had no idea she was interested in my climb.

Roxi's birthday was today! We had celebrated Cheryl's birthday a couple of weeks ago in fine style, so a certain standard had been set. Roxi and Robyn wore sparkly boas and crazy sunglasses to dinner in the mess tent. Victor and I tried on joke glasses with spirals for "lenses," while the rest of the team writhed with laughter. Phil, good sport that he was, let Roxi and Robyn dress him in a glittery tube top, sparkly boa, and sunglasses with star-shaped lenses. We teased him about his secret life and what his wife would say when she saw the pictures. Chhongba produced a luscious birthday cake with lit candles. Cheryl and Nikki gave Roxi a wrapped package, while Laurel struck up the iPod orchestra. We played Pass the Parcel. When the music stopped, whoever was holding the package removed a layer of wrapping. We timed it so that Roxi got to remove the last layer. Inside was a tiny case the size of a lipstick containing miniature tweezers, mirror, and a light. There was an awkward pause, while Roxi teared up.

Suddenly, perhaps to mask her tears, Roxi grabbed a startled Dendi Sherpa, our assistant cook, and danced a mad tango with him, camp chairs tumbling in their wake. Dendi, recovering from his surprise, grinned broadly, as Roxi planted a big kiss on his cheek. "Nothing for his wife to worry about," someone chuckled. The other Sherpas grinned at this Western madness. We finished off a wonderful day by watching "Monty Python and the Holy Grail" in the mess tent. After the movie I was in my sleeping bag by 8:30 pm, unheard of back home. Ah, the life of a mountaineer!

April 23. Laurel and Simon were feeling camp bound and keen to take a walk beyond Base Camp. Roxi, Robyn, and I joined them. We hiked to Pumori Base Camp and had a picnic on a blanket among some boulders. Robyn and Laurel lay on their backs and entertained us by doing odd things with their toes. Robyn was wearing her sparkly blue boa from her mom's birthday party. I could not remember the last time I took time to sit in the sun and hang out with friends like this. Pleasant as it was, a chilly breeze urged me to get moving before the others were ready to leave. I picked my way down a steep slope of talus and across the steep boulder-strewn trough to the ridge leading back to Base Camp.

Afternoon snow squalls blew up the valley, as I returned to Base Camp. I put on warmer clothes and joined a lively game of Black Jack in the mess tent. Mark Cohen was dealer and banker; currency was packets of apple cider drink and pralines. I usually am not much of a card player, but Mark's lively patter, Phil's steely stare, and Heddwyn's and Lydia's wise cracks were lots of fun. Afterwards I helped the Sherpas level Mike's tent site.

Another mountain guide, Kenton Cool, and his client climber, Ran, joined us for dinner. Steve had heard Ran give a talk in England. Talking with Ran, Steve smiled and laughed more than he had for days. Mark took several pictures. Later I learned Ran was a famous adventurer and philanthropist who had been knighted.

During our dinner conversation, Kenton reported that the Olympic Torch had arrived at Advanced Base Camp on the Tibet side of Everest. If the torch relay team summits soon, maybe the restrictions on our own climbing will end. We might get to climb this mountain yet.

April 24. This evening we had a team meeting in the mess tent. We were all seated along the long dining table when Mike entered. Mark queued up "Hail to the Chief" on the iPod. Robyn used a tomato sauce bottle as a microphone to introduce him. We applauded. Mike tolerated our silliness with patient good humor.

Mike summarized the latest restrictions. No one would be allowed to climb past Camp 2. Armed guards would enforce this restriction; they would shoot violators. The military could show up unannounced, search our tents, and demand that we share our food with them without compensation. As if these issues were not enough trouble, a toilet war was raging. Members of the military had stood on some of the Camp 2 toilets and crapped all over them, making them unusable. Yesterday's collective optimism about the Olympic Torch's progress abruptly shifted to indignation and frustration. The next few days of uncertain waiting were maddening.

The Armed Camp

April 25. After two restless days in Base Camp, we were up at 3:30 am, back in climber mode. Mike had decided that we would climb to Camp 2, at elevation 20,800 feet, in spite of the draconian restrictions there. Tendi and I left Base Camp at 4:30 am. We reached the first ladder bridges in just over an hour, a personal best for me. We climbed through the Popcorn, the Soccer Field (a relatively flat area), more Popcorn, crossing about 35 ladder bridges, climbed up the wall ladders, and through the big crevasses. We arrived at Camp 1 at 10:15 am, another personal best for me, just behind Steve and Lydia. I was still slow and became quite breathless while climbing up steep pitches, but I recovered quickly during short rest breaks. Perhaps I was acclimatizing and getting stronger after all.

At Camp 1 I ducked into my sleeping tent to get out of the brilliant sun. My pack thermometer read 100 degrees Fahrenheit. Drowning in sweat, I opened the tent's ventilation zippers, stripped to briefs and bra, and sprawled on top of my minus 40 degrees down sleeping bag. I chugged water every few minutes, but the heat seemed to strip moisture from my body faster than I could replace it. I drank, wrote in my journal, read, and dozed. When the sun went down behind the mountains, the temperature plummeted to below freezing. I hustled back into layers of warm clothing.

April 26. After a breakfast of two packets of instant oatmeal, two packets of hot chocolate, and two mugs of hot lemon tea, Tendi and I left at 7:45 am for Camp 2. The route now went around most of the wide crevasses we had climbed through the last time we were up here. Mike said this more circuitous route was the proper route, and conditions were the most favorable he had seen. In contrast to the many ladder bridges in the Icefall, we had to cross only six bridges between Camp 1 and Camp 2. Some of the young Sherpas returning from Camp 2 ran across them with youthful abandon, as the ladders bounced and clanged alarmingly. I still took deep slow breaths to calm my anxiety at each bridge, placed each foot carefully, and crossed as a snail's pace.

At about 10 am, we could see tents ahead perched on a ridge of loose dark rock on climber's left above us as we moved up the Western Cwm. It seemed to take long time before the tents looked any closer. The route wove around the biggest crevasses, first to climber's right, then to climber's left. We finally reached the first tents in Camp 2, then we climbed past them up a narrow gully of rock and ice. Passang Sherpa met us in the gully with a kettle of cold instant mango drink. I sat and drank two cups of it plus two cups of water. Though I had no appetite, I dutifully chewed nuts, raisins, and Gummi Bears. Energy flowed back into my body.

Suddenly I started to cough. I tried to stop but could not. I coughed so hard that I wretched and nearly lost the fluids and calories I had just taken in. Breaking ribs from high altitude coughing fits is not uncommon. "You OK?," Lydia asked, an edge of concern in her voice. "Yeah," I croaked weakly, staring at the blood-streaked phlegm I had just coughed onto the rocks near my boots. "No problem," I said, trying to reassure myself as well as Lydia. We all have been coughing up this stuff. No big deal. Still unnerved, I stood on trembling legs, shouldered my pack, and headed up the gully, trying not to stumble over loose rock or slip on the ice. I cursed the fact that our tents were at the far end of Camp 2. Later

I realized our tents were ideally located, beyond and above the waste from other expeditions.

On a rocky ridge above the Western Cwm, Camp 2 had some of the comforts of Base Camp, including a small mess tent with a dining table and chairs as well as a toilet tent with a "throne." Zangbu Sherpa would cook for us here. These amenities were intended to provide comfort and appealing meals, so we could rest and eat well here before climbing higher on the mountain.

Even with these amenities, Camp 2 was not very appealing. Our tents were scattered among dark boulders, loose rock, dirty ice, and trash left by other expeditions. At an elevation of nearly 21,000 feet, the short downhill walk from my sleeping tent to the mess tent left me breathless and feeling lousy. We had been told the military's armed guards would shoot anyone who tried to climb toward Camp 3. Though I did not see any weapons, Camp 2 felt like an armed prison camp.

Today Zangbu pulled out the stops for lunch: cheese, whole-grain crackers, burritos, and cookies, a great change from the standard Camp 1 fare of tomato sauce and chapattis. I wished my appetite were better, so I could do Zangbu's special lunch justice. That afternoon, we retired to our sleeping tents to read, nap, and acclimatize to the new high altitude. I made myself as comfortable as possible. Down booties kept my feet wonderfully warm inside my sleeping bag. They also made nice "socks" inside my outer mountaineering boots for short walks around camp.

April 27. We had a lazy morning in camp. Zangbu made a big rest day breakfast. I still had little appetite and did not want to eat. However, I remembered Guy Cotter's advice about setting goals for eating. I put a dab of scrambled eggs in my bowl, ignored the fatty bacon, and added a piece of toast and a few cashews. It took over an hour, but I made myself eat everything in my bowl. Every bite was an act of sheer will. To distract my queasy stomach, I listened intently while Victor told us about some of his challenging climbs.

I tried to get Lydia to talk about her impressive climb of Everest without supplemental oxygen 20 years ago.

Since the military would not permit us to climb beyond Camp 2, Mike suggested we take an acclimatization hike up the black talus slope behind our tents. I still felt lousy and tired. At first I decided to rest in camp. Then I thought perhaps I would feel better, if I did the hike. The others already had started, so I went at my own slow pace following their route across a frozen pond, around crevasses, and past seracs. This is good, I told myself, I won't be tempted to keep up with them. Ironically, I passed Victor, Cheryl and Nikki, each of whom was carrying two oxygen cylinders in their packs as practice for climbing higher on the mountain. I was impressed and felt guilty that I was not carrying a heavier pack. I passed Robyn and Phil and joined Lydia, Mike, and Ang Dorje who were sitting on a rocky point.

We enjoyed the cool thin sunshine and the views of the now familiar Western Cwm below us. The Cwm was a long stretch of white glacier, walled on both sides by mountains of dark rock, snow and ice, running from the top of the Khumbu Icefall, which we had climbed, to the base of the Lhotse Face, which we would climb. The climb down the talus from our rocky point was a bit tricky in big mountaineering boots, but it went well without any embarrassing falls. We were back in camp within two hours. I felt better. I was glad I had gone for this little hike. It is sometimes difficult to know when to push through discomfort and when to rest. This time I made the right choice.

April 28. At 5:45 am, it was 15 degrees Fahrenheit, but it felt colder. I was tired of the wind, cold, and the effort needed to do the most basic tasks, like getting up to go to the toilet tent, at nearly 21,000 feet elevation. I felt better, after I had dressed and tramped around camp. After breakfast, a noisy card game began in the mess tent. Mike, Victor, Lydia, Hedd-wyn, a visitor named Marty, and I traded stories, shouting over the card game. Perhaps the loudness was my team mates' way of blowing off nervous energy or frustration, but the noise made my head hurt.

After lunch some of us climbed the black talus slope again. I was nervous about dropping and damaging the cylinders of compressed oxygen, so I carried a three-person tent instead. We leaned into the wind and found our footing across the ice pond, past the seracs, and up the talus. I took an embarrassing fall on the pond, but no one saw it, so maybe it did not count. Again we sat above Camp 2 for awhile on the rocky point, then slipped and slid back down in the talus and ice.

In my sleeping tent, I finished reading "The Bell Jar and the Butterfly," Bauby's autobiography about being severely incapacitated by a stroke as a relatively young man and living as boldly as his condition allowed. It helped me put my own concerns about being too slow and old in perspective. I felt very lucky to be here on Everest and able to do what I can do.

Solitude and Camaraderie

April 29. At 5:30 am it was very cold and windy. Today we would climb down to Base Camp. I stored gear to stay at Camp 2. I dressed for climbing down through the Icefall in a Gore-Tex mountaineering jacket and ice climbing bibs over a base layer and insulating layers, climbing harness, and mountaineering boots. I shuffled to the mess tent feeling bulky and awkward. I choked down two small pancakes, bacon from which I had pulled off strips of fat, and drank two cups of hot water. It was time to add layers of clothing, brave the cold, and descend through the Icefall.

Tendi and I made good time from Camp 2 to Camp 1. The sun was well up now. Heat had replaced this morning's numbing cold. I stripped off layers of clothing and put on sun screen and glacier goggles. By then, Robyn, Phil, and Lydia had already started down the Icefall. As we wove through the maze of seracs and crevasses, Tendi helped untangle me, when I caught my pack on fixed lines that we had to pass under. He checked my safety carabiner and scolded me, when I did not attach it properly to the fixed line after passing a piece of protection. When I struggled to pass my ascender while wearing my thick mountaineering gloves, Tendi sometimes did it for me. I felt humiliated. I thought I should be able to do it myself, but I appreciated his keeping me safe.

Carol Masheter crossing a ladder bridge, while Tendi Sherpa kept the safety lines tight, April 29, 2008, photo by Lydia Bradey.

After about 5 hours, we reached the base of the Icefall. Mark and Laurel met us at the training area with Cokes. Lydia, who had already dropped off her pack in Base Camp, joined us. Lydia and Laurel each gave me a big welcome hug. After a short rest, Tendi and I shambled up the last talus slope to Base Camp, where Ang Tsering and the camp Sherpas smiled their welcome. With their gold teeth and bling, I felt as though I were on a movie set for "Pirates of the Caribbean."

After a much anticipated hot shower, I realized how much better I felt in Base Camp than at Camp 2. Chhongba had outdone himself again with a splendid lunch of sushi, mo mos (Tibetan dumplings with vegetable or meat filling), sliced fresh tomatoes and cucumbers, diced apples and oranges in strawberry yogurt. My appetite was back, and I could enjoy this wonderful spread.

Base Camp had changed. While we were away, ice had melted and shifted under our tents. Camp Sherpas had releveled our tent sites and improved the stone walk ways. Even the stone "steps" to my sleeping tent had been rebuilt.

April 30. This morning, while we were eating breakfast in the sun, a white plane flew slowly over Base Camp, wheeled, and flew over us again. Our guides thought it was a Chinese surveillance plane. They had also heard from the military that everyone must be down from Camp 1 and 2 by tomorrow. Our guides were glad we had come down yesterday, avoiding the stampede and the added risk of falling ice from a lot of people climbing down in a hurry. I hoped the restrictions on our climbing activities meant the Chinese would soon summit with the Olympic Torch, the restrictions would be lifted, and we could resume climbing higher on the mountain.

As Passang was helping me reposition my drying laundry in the fickle sunshine, a big helicopter wop-wopped into Base Camp. It hovered several hundred feet from our cluster of tents. Several men swarmed around the 'copter, its rotors still whirling in the thin air. They looked like soldiers. According to rumors, more soldiers would arrive tomorrow. It was unnerving.

May 1. We still had to complete at least one more acclimatization cycle to Camp 3 at nearly 24,000 feet elevation, before we would be ready for our summit climb. However the military would not let us climb above Base Camp now. Mike decided we would go back down to Pheriche for a few days. There, at about 14,000 feet elevation, we could fatten up and rest before climbing up to Camp 3. I considered staying in Base Camp. I trusted Chhongba's cooking more than the food in Pheriche. However the rest of the team was leaving for Pheriche, so I made preparations to go too.

May 4. I could take only so much rest and waiting in Pheriche. Since we had arrived three days ago, I had gone to the clinic and heard the educational talk about high altitude problems from the young physician in residence. I had walked up and down the dusty paths through the village countless times. Bored and restless, I got the OK from Mike to take an acclimatization hike on my own. I wanted to hike up to a pointed peak that Simon had climbed yesterday. Mike suggested a less ambitious walk to Dengboche, a village a couple of valleys away. Fueled by a vegetable omelet, canned fruit, and slices of fresh apple, I left the White Yak Lodge before the others were up. I headed down the valley, frost crackling under my leather hiking boots. Wearing them was a welcome change from my bulky mountaineering boots. As I hiked down the valley I found the pointed mountain irresistible and headed up it instead of toward Dengboche.

Clouds rolled up the valley, and snow squalls threatened. I decided to see how far I could get before the weather turned bad. First, I needed to find a safe way across a swift stream. I found a rickety plywood bridge and crossed it, then climbed up a brown, barren ridge. I turned around and looked down on a patchwork of stone-walled yak pens. I continued up a large steep brown hill past herds of grazing yaks and rocky outcroppings. Tiny jewel-like alpine flowers were starting to bloom. The smell of growing things was tantalizing after weeks on the glacier.

About two thirds of the way up, I stopped, sat on a rock, and looked back the way I had come. I spotted a distant energetic figure climbing up toward me. As the figure approached, I realized it was Mike. Uh oh, I'm busted. Will he be annoyed that I came up here when he suggested Dengboche instead?

Mike joined me at my rock. He seemed OK with my mutiny. I asked him if he wanted company, as we continued up. He said no, he wanted to hike alone. I felt a small pang of rejection, but with all the drama of military restrictions and patience wearing thin among some members of our group, I could understand his need for solitude. He was faster than me anyway. If we agreed to hike separately, I would not be tempted to try to keep up with him. Slow steady hiking would be better for my acclimatization, I told myself. I watched his orange jacket bob and weave up through the rocky crags to the summit. Mike passed me on his way down. He said, "Only 20 minutes to the top and well worth it."

When I summited 10 minutes later, I felt a sense of childish pride that I had reached the top in half the time Mike had estimated. Then my pride segued to wonder. Snowflakes sparkled and swirled around me like fairy dust among strings of fluttering blue, red, green, yellow, and white prayer flags. The mountain fell away at my feet in a sheer drop of many hundreds of feet, a drop that could not be seen from the direction I had climbed. This felt like a magical place. As I gazed around, taking in the beauty, I spotted Mike's woolly hat about 20 feet down a steep drop among the rocks. I carefully climbed down and retrieved it. I noticed the snow was falling more thickly. It was time to leave, before the weather deteriorated further.

As I picked my way down through the rocks, I startled a quartet of immature Nepali pheasants, which took flight and sailed down and out of sight behind a ridge. Lower down, a flock of doves exploded into flight and wheeled in unison, their wings flashing in the intermittent sunshine. I heard occasional bird song and distant yak bells. I exchanged namastes with a Sherpani tending her grazing yaks on the hillside. Though my watch indicated I was making much better time going down than climbing up, my descent seemed to take a long time. I glanced nervously at the sky, as I tried to speed up my pace. Down at the stream I crossed the plywood bridge. Not long afterwards, I met a large group of hikers who were looking for a way to cross safely, so I led them back to the bridge. As I returned to the White Yak Lodge, I felt very pleased with my walk, an estimated 2,500 feet elevation gain. I found Mike and returned his hat. "Well done," he said with a grin.

May 5. As a break from the heavy duties of eating, sleeping, and reading, I took a walk to Dengboche. The sky was overcast and leaden. Any photographs would probably be dull and dark, so I concentrated on making mental memories. I crested the first ridge behind the White Yak Lodge, then two more ridges. I came downhill past old white chortens joined to the village by long strings of prayer flags.

Dengboche was busier and more colorful than Pheriche. A steady stream of hikers, local people, and yaks thronged the main path past lodges, shops, and a lumber yard where men were using a two-man saw to cut a log into boards. Others were constructing new buildings with hand-quarried blocks of stone and wooden timbers. A tall young Sherpa stopped me, "Namaste, Didi, I am Phurba Sherpa," he said, eyeing my powder-blue Adventure Consultants jacket. Please say hi to Lydia Didi for me." I grinned and promised to pass on his message. A Sherpa in Nepal could pass a verbal greeting to a guide from New Zealand via a woman from the United States. It was a small world.

I walked through Dengboche and past a few stone-walled garden plots then headed back toward Pheriche. A black and tan dog trotted ahead of me for awhile, before it headed off on its own canine business. I crossed a couple of low rocky ridges then spotted an energetic figure scrambling up a distant boulder. I bet it was Victor. Sure enough, as I got nearer, I could see Victor and several guys from another expedition bouldering (climbing without harness or rope on large boulders or low on rock faces). They all were better climbers than I, so I watched and praised their skill. Finally they persuaded me to try an easy pitch in my hiking boots. They cheered as I found my holds and propelled myself awkwardly up the boulder. I felt like one of the gang. It was a nice feeling.

I climbed with the guys, until the overcast sky darkened and threatened snow. They wanted to keep climbing, but I headed for the White Yak Lodge. I arrived just as the first snow flakes swirled and thickened into a squall. I hoped the guys would not get too wet and cold.

From inside the sun room at the White Yak, I watched the snow, wind, and rain play chase outside. Now that we were away from Base Camp, the military restrictions on email did not apply. I emailed my sister and friends back home and reassured them that all was well without using any words forbidden by the military, just to be on the safe side. The clouds broke up and alpine glow turned the new snow peach-colored on the surrounding peaks. Outside two little stallions squealed and stamped at each other over a stone wall like quarrelling children.

Rescue

After dinner, we received word that one of our Base Camp Sherpas was seriously ill. He was being carried down from Base Camp to the Pheriche clinic by a team of Sherpas. Victor and Simon grabbed their packs and headed up to meet them. Lydia and I looked franticly for her missing radio. I loaned her my headlamp, so she could follow Victor and Simon and take event notes about the stricken Sherpa's condition. The rest of us were instructed to stay in Pheriche.

I wanted to help. I decided to take a large thermos of tea to the Pheriche clinic for the rescue party, when they arrived. I asked Pema, one of our cook's helpers, to prepare the tea. It seemed to take forever. Meanwhile, I loaded my pack with clean mugs and an extra jacket, hat, and gloves in case the wait outside the clinic for the rescue party was long and cold.

Several of us milled around restlessly outside the clinic, waiting in the dark. Every noise sounded like the approaching rescue party. A young Belgian woman, who was the on-duty physician at the clinic, asked me repeatedly about the sick Sherpa's condition. I told her what little I knew, that the Sherpa was unresponsive and was being carried down from Base Camp. Nikki showed up and told her that our expedition physician was meeting the rescue party. He would be able to tell her more, when they arrived.

At last, many shuffling feet and a chorus of coughing announced the rescue party's arrival. A young man, Tashi Thundu Sherpa, was wrapped in blankets and strapped to a ladder serving as a stretcher. His eyes were closed, and his face was an alarming shade of gray. At least 20 other Sherpas had helped carry him down the rocky trail from Base Camp. Some of them stumbled, as they carried Tashi Thundu into the clinic. Two Sherpanis, who also had thermoses, and I passed among the rescuers, handing them steaming mugs of tea. Cheryl and Nikki followed with the cookies. Tired faces creased into weary smiles of thanks. I recognized Dendi among the stretcher bearers. His smooth brown face was solemn. "Long carry," I said. "No problem," he replied softly.

I could smell alcohol among the rescuers. I was shocked. Carrying a stretcher down that trail in the daylight while sober would have been hard enough. These guys did it in the dark, and some of them were drunk. Later we learned the rescued Sherpa's diagnosis was acute gastritis brought on by alcohol abuse. Apparently, some of the Base Camp Sherpas had been drinking heavily, while we were in Pheriche. I fought my impulse to be judgmental – and lost. Sherpa lives seemed hard and dangerous enough without alcohol abuse.

May 6. Today we would return to Base Camp. Several days ago I had been reluctant to come down to Pheriche. Now I was sad to leave the White Yak Lodge. It had been warm and comfortable. I had enjoyed my walks above Pheriche and had gained strength and confidence. However, staying in Pheriche would not get me to the summit.

The morning started with a helicopter evacuation of Tashi Thundu. After he was helped aboard, he needed to deplane to vomit. He was afraid of flying in the helicopter. Roxi had decided to leave the expedition, so she would fly with him to Kathmandu. She said she would hold his hand. For a moment, I envied Roxi. She would ride elephants and look for tigers in the lowlands of Nepal. Right now that sounded a lot more fun than climbing Everest.

The walk from Pheriche to Lobuche went quickly. Some of us stopped in Lobuche for lunch. I spotted Jason, a tall shaggy-haired young man I had met weeks ago during our hike from Lukla to Base Camp. He was taking a break from teaching English to monks at a nearby monastery. He, his friend, Hillary, and I shared fresh tomato and cheese sandwiches.

The rest of our group showed no signs of leaving, so I got the okay from Mike to go ahead on my own. Along the long boulder-strewn trail, the usual steady trickle of climbers, hikers, porters, yak pack trains, and their handlers crept ahead in a zigzag line of dancing specks of color. Every hour I stopped for a few minutes of self-care, as we did as a group. At times, the route did not look familiar, and I could not see anyone else. I felt a few pangs of anxiety. Am I lost?

Then a yak carrying my purple duffel bag passed me, so I could not be very lost. Finally, I saw the distinctive light and dark layered mountain behind Base Camp. A few minutes of hiking later, I could make out the tiny flecks of color among the vast expanse of boulders, rocks, and ice. The flecks of color were the dozens of tents that made up Base Camp. I was relieved.

The trail became familiar again. I descended the steep downhill before the undulating rocky ridge with its forest of fanciful cairns and crossed the trough before the first tents on the edges of Base Camp. As usual, our camp crew welcomed us warmly. Ang Tsering and Chhongba had become my Sherpa uncles, though I was older than both of them.

In the mess tent, we learned that Hedd-wyn had been diagnosed with High Altitude Pulmonary Edema (HAPE) and would stay with Simon in Lobuche tonight. My heart sank. HAPE is serious. Also, Hedd-wyn had lost his camera. Such bad luck! Hedd-wyn had been so energetic, positive, and strong up to now. I fervently hoped he would recover and be able to climb with the rest of us.

May 7. At 5:20 am, the interior of my sleeping tent sparkled with frost. I dressed carefully, avoiding the frosty tent walls, which dumped ice crystals down my neck when I touched them. No one was stirring, so after a quiet foggy morning stroll through Base Camp, I went back to my tent and read and dozed in my sleeping bag. The fog burned off. A typical leisurely rest day followed, complete with Chhongba's tomato, onion, and mushroom omelets for breakfast. Some of us dined outside in the thin sunshine.

The news circulating through Base Camp was grim. Strong winds on the Tibetan side of Everest had destroyed some of the tents for Chinese Olympic torch relay team, causing their summit attempt to fail. Now what? Will the Chinese give up? Not likely, with the eyes of the world on the Olympic Torch relay, I thought gloomily. More restrictions and delays were more probable. The good weather we had enjoyed for so many weeks seemed unlikely to continue long enough for us to summit.

There was more bad news. Back in New Zealand, the media had interviewed Guy Cotter about the restrictions on Everest. Some of Guy Cotter's comments had been taken out of context. Now the Nepalese military was focusing its attention on our Adventure Consultants expedition. Our liaison officer was too embarrassed to come to our mess tent for several days. Though I did not miss his awkward presence at meals, I was surprised by it. I imagined the officer would want to keep an eye on us, if we were supposed to be such troublemakers.

I felt sick with discouragement. The restrictions by the Chinese, enforced by the Nepalese military, seemed so irrational and unpredictable. At this rate, we were never going get a chance to climb this mountain.

During a team meeting in the mess tent, Mike said personality clashes had flared within our group. He asked us to be patient. We had only three or four more weeks together. One team member and I had had our rough moments, but that had been weeks ago. I was not sure who else was upset with whom, but I had read accounts about conflicts among expedition members that led to disastrous results, even deaths. Climbing big mountains pushes many people to their limits, bringing out the worst as well as the best. We had to be able to work together, even if we did not always like each other. I resolved to be part of the solution rather than part of the problem.

May 8. At breakfast we heard the Olympic Torch had reached the summit. The collective dark mood of last night dissipated like smoke in a stiff breeze. Excitement raced through Base Camp like electricity. Soldiers in Base Camp and in camps higher on the mountain had been sick with altitude and GI problems, since they had arrived. They could not wait to leave Base Camp for more comfortable surroundings. Soldiers were packing like mad to race down the mountain, while expeditions were packing like mad to race up the mountain. It was like a high-spirited screwball comedy.

With so many climbers moving up the mountain, Mike decided we would wait in Base Camp for a few days. We all were impatient to climb, but waiting seemed like a good idea to me. I did not like the heightened risk of being hit by falling ice knocked loose by other climbers or getting stuck in long cold traffic jams high on the mountain.

May 9. Victor, Cheryl, and Nikki left for Camp 1 today. The rest of us stayed in Base Camp for another rest day. To celebrate the lifting of the military restrictions, I hiked part way up Pumori. Spring was awakening some of the carpet-like alpine plants. The air smelled spicy and alive. I picked my way up through boulders and loose rock to a large cairn on a high ridge. When I looked back beyond Base Camp toward Everest, I noticed a stripe of vivid colors in the sky, an upside down rainbow without rain, its ends curving up slightly like the Mona Lisa's mysterious smile. I had seen sundogs back home in Utah, but I had never seen anything like this. I was eager to return to Base Camp and ask whether any of the others have seen it.

In camp I went to the mess tent to pack enough snacks for several days of climbing up to Camp 3. Over the weeks, I had learned some things that tasted good to me in Base Camp were not appealing higher on the mountain. Chocolate, which I usually liked, tasted like wax up high. "Fox food," my own mix of dried fruit, nuts, and M &

Ms, which I usually liked, made me gag, when I tried to eat it above 20,000 feet elevation. Mike had told us Gummi Bears would stay soft enough to eat in the cold, but I could not find any among the assorted snacks. I did not want to run low on calories up high, but I did not want carry more than I could eat. At high altitude, every ounce has seemed to weigh a pound. Anything I did not eat, I would have to carry back down.

In the afternoon some of us took a break from packing for the summit climb and watched the movie, "Bucket List," in the mess tent. This feel-good movie about two terminally ill guys who are doing all the things they want to do in life before they "kicked the bucket" was a perfect movie for me to see before our summit climb. After a delicious dinner of chicken curry, couscous, peas, beans, and instant cheese cake, I settled into my sleeping bag. Tomorrow we would climb to Camp 1. I tried not to worry about the climbing through the Icefall with its teetering seracs and wobbly ladder bridges.

The Lhotse Face

May 10. As usual, it was below freezing and dark at 4:30 am, when Tendi and I were ready to leave Base Camp. By now our routine had become well practiced. After a Spartan breakfast of cold cereal and fruit, we shouldered our packs and tossed rice at the puja altar, as we passed it on our right. We crunched across the narrow frozen lakes and climbed up and down the ice ridges of Lower Lake Lands, then crossed the many ladder bridges in the Popcorn. As usual, most of the others in our expedition passed us. I saw Ang Dorje pause to pray and toss a few grains of rice blessed by Lama Geshe into a particularly nasty looking crevasse. His concern aroused some of my anxiety demons. I firmly told the demons to get lost.

The fixed lines were icy today. My gloves got wet and then froze, making my hands too cold and stiff to operate my ascender. At one of our rest stops I changed into dry gloves. My hands soon felt better. I was relieved to have solved the cold hands problem, but ligaments in my pelvis hurt, something I had noticed during yesterday's hike to Pumori Base Camp. I did not know how to solve that problem. I hoped the pain would not get worse. Aging is not for sissies, I thought wryly.

High in the Icefall, two icefall doctors were replacing ladder bridges damaged by the shifting glacier. They looked up and stared at me glassy-eyed, as I thanked them for their work. The stink of cheap alcohol swept over me. Apparently the icefall doctors had been drinking. I worried about their safety as well as the quality of their work, upon which other lives depended. I tried to think beyond my negative judgments. I wondered whether the icefall doctors drank to numb their fear of the Icefall's dangers. Certainly I could relate to that. Even after several climbs through it, I found the Icefall a beautiful but terrifying place.

I felt triumphant and relieved, when we climbed the last wall ladder near the top of the Icefall. We climbed down into and up out of the giant crevasses toward Camp 1. The sun beat down, turning the Western Cwm into a giant reflector oven. I stripped off as many layers as possible without exposing skin to the brutal rays. I felt like a prospector lost in a scorching desert, as I plodded through the shimmering heat. The only climbers I passed today were a tall elderly Nepalese gentleman and a group of young women from Singapore who seemed even more exhausted then I. Later I learned the elderly man became the oldest person to summit Everest about two weeks later. After nearly six hours of climbing I dragged into Camp 1 about 45 minutes after my team mates. I had hoped to be stronger, faster, and more able to keep up with the rest of the team after living on this mountain for a month. I tried not to let discouragement trump the triumph I had felt at the top of the Icefall.

Mike, Lydia, Robyn, Phil, and Hedd-wyn were sitting on their Z-rests (foldable closed-cell sleeping mats), resting in the sun and drinking tea. As I shuffled wearily toward them, they shouted cheery welcomes and invited me to join their "beach party." I did not feel much like partying, but I got my Z-rest and joined them. Their lively welcome and a mug of tea lifted my spirits. As intermittent clouds raced overhead, we alternated between roasting and freezing, putting on and taking off hats, gloves, and jackets. Climbers from other expeditions greeted us, as they trudged on to Camp 2. "I'm shattered," grinned Trumpy, a young climber with another expedition. Far from appearing shattered, he seemed to have more energy climbing than I had lounging on my Z-rest. As he strode past us on young springy legs, I felt old and tired. I was glad our climbing was done for today.

Afternoon snow showers rolled in, so we retreated to our sleeping tents. I opened a bottle of Ensure, a liquid nutritional supplement, and drank it hoping that it would increase my energy for tomorrow's climb to Camp 2. Then I settled into my sleeping bag for an afternoon of reading and writing, listening to the hiss of snow blowing against my tent walls. I felt very snug and comfortable, even as several loud avalanches thundered down the mountains flanking the Western Cwm.

May 12. Today we planned to climb from Camp 2 to the base of the Lhotse Face and up its first few hundred feet. I chose my clothing carefully: base layer top and bottoms, Schoeller glacier pants, lined Marmot wind jacket, Mountain Hardwear Compression jacket, balaclava, liner gloves, and thick Black Diamond Guide gloves.

I was worried about climbing the Lhotse Face. People have fallen to their death from a single careless step. Lydia reassured me the Face was not as steep as it looked. "You're strong," she said, "You'll make it. Take two breaths for every step. I'll climb with you." I appreciated her encouragement, because I did not feel strong today. I knew I would need more than two breaths per step, but I was afraid if I told Lydia, my chances for a place on the summit team would vanish.

In the mess tent, eating breakfast was a sheer act of will. Everything made me want to vomit. If I took small bites and chewed slowly, the food stayed down. I managed to eat two small pancakes with syrup and a small serving of scrambled eggs in about half an hour. Because we were moving to a higher altitude, I took half a pill of Diamox, about 125 milligrams. Tendi offered to carry my pack. I would need to carry my own pack on summit day and should practice, but I did not want to confuse him. Reluctantly I let him carry my pack today.

As we left Camp 2, I felt OK. I was a little chilly but not too cold, the way I liked to feel when I started a climb. As we moved up the Western Cwm, the wind increased. It sliced through my clothing layers and numbed me to the bone. After about an hour, Lydia asked me if I was OK. "I'm really c-c-cold," I muttered. My face was so stiff I could barely speak. My hands were as stiff and useless as blocks of wood. I felt sluggish, withdrawn, and cranky. Tendi helped me pull my Gore-Tex ski jacket from my pack. I had not brought my big down parka, because I did not think I would need it. Lydia gave me a well-deserved scolding for leaving it at Camp 2. She loaned me her mid-weight down jacket, and we resumed climbing toward the Lhotse Face. Within 15 minutes I felt better. Lydia's loaned jacket did the trick. I was grateful for her generosity.

I found a rhythm of two breaths per step. I was slow but steady. We caught up with the others, who were sitting and resting near the base of the Lhotse Face. We had to cross a crevasse and then climb steep hard ice, the first bit of the Face.

Mike gave us last minute advice. "Make every step solid. Jab as many points of your crampons into the ice as possible." He added that climbing a little way up the Face today was optional. It looked really scary. Phil had had enough for today and turned back with Lydia. I was tempted to turn back with them. Mike and Hedd-wyn headed up the Face. As I watched them, I heard myself say to Tendi, "Let's go up a ways." He nodded. I stowed my hiking poles, put on my climbing helmet, and took a couple of deep breaths to steady my nerves.

We jumped across the crevasse at the base of the Face, clipped onto the fixed line, and climbed. I focused on where to place my feet, looking for places where I could bite the ice with as many of my crampon points as possible. I found my rhythm: take a step, take four breaths, slide my safety and ascender up the fixed line, repeat the cycle. I was slow but steady. My fear of falling down the infamous Lhotse Face still lurked like some menacing beast in the back of my mind, but my fear was manageable. The climbing was far from the most technically difficult climbing I had ever done, but it was very hard work to make my body, dulled by thin cold air, do what it knew how to do. We climbed a few hundred vertical feet up to a small ledge. I felt encouraged. Today was not as hard or scary as I had feared.

Back in Camp 2, I sat on a boulder in the sun and chatted with Lydia, Mike, Hedd-wyn, and Phil. Zhangbu brought us cold mango drink and cookies. The sugar rush and the small triumph of today's climb flooded me with warmth and confidence. I felt like a new woman. I could climb this mountain!

May 13. Cheryl, Nikki, and Victor had spent a cold windy night at Camp 3 at nearly 24,000 feet without supplemental oxygen. When they returned to Camp 2, they were in good spirits in spite of not sleeping much. Today it was our turn. If they can do it, I can do it, I chanted to myself, trying to override my rising anxiety and self-doubt.

When we left Camp 2, I wore my big down parka over my other layers of clothing. It was too warm, but I had learned a hard lesson yesterday and did not want to risk hypothermia again. I carried my own pack, since we planned to sleep at Camp 3 tonight, and Tendi's pack was full of his own overnight gear.

From Camp 2, we could see the tents of Camp 3, dots of color arranged on giant shelves in the Lhotse Face. Our tents were on the highest shelf, at Upper Camp 3. As we climbed up the Western Cwm, the wind was stronger than it was yesterday. I was glad to be wearing many layers, though they made me felt bulky and awkward.

I was very slow today. I stumbled heavily up and over the smallest ice ridges. Climbing the bigger ridges felt like torture, as I fought to extract enough oxygen from the thin cold air and find solid foot placements. As we neared the Lhotse Face, wind roared down it, transporting snow in a ghostly veil that made the Face seem to crawl. It reminded me of footage in Everest documentaries over which the narrator grimly recited the deadly dangers of climbing this mountain. Between glances up the Face, I ducked my head and face into my parka like a turtle to avoid the bite of the wind and the cold that burned any exposed skin like liquid nitrogen.

When Tendi and I got to the base of the Face, yesterday's new confidence evaporated like frost in sunshine. I was terrified. The wind-driven snow pouring down the Face mesmerized me and made me dizzy. I fought the urge to vomit. I tried to steady my breathing, but it remained ragged and uneven. A battle raged inside me. If I collapsed while climbing the Face, I would put Tendi, as well as myself, in extreme danger. Before this trip I had vowed that I would turn back rather than risk someone else's life unnecessarily. However, months ago Guy Cotter had made it clear that everyone who wanted to try for the summit must first climb the Lhotse Face and sleep a night at Camp 3 without supplemental oxygen. If I did not accomplish this, I would not get a spot on the summit team. Climb up or go back, climb or go back, I argued with myself. I heard myself saying, "Tendi Bai, we should go back. I don't feel well. I don't want to put you in danger." Tendi nodded impassively and turned around to descend.

With a heavy sense of defeat, I followed Tendi back to Camp 2. Dark thoughts swirled through my head like sinister birds of prey. If I cannot climb the Lhotse Face, I cannot climb to the summit of Everest. How would I face people back home? I imagined having to tell them, one by one. I could feel each little moment of shame. I could hear them saying to each other, "What was she thinking, trying to climb Everest? She is too old and too slow."

Of course, most of my friends would not have said any of these things and probably would not have even thought them. Sometimes my drive to do something outstanding and my failure to achieve my self-imposed high standards have been my worst enemies. Summiting to impress people is not a very good reason to climb Everest, I reminded myself. I came here to see what this mountain has to teach me. Then my childish pride piped up, but I still would like to summit.

As we neared Camp 2, we met Paul Rogers, otherwise known as Dodgy, a guide who was leading clients up the neighboring peak, Lhotse. He greeted us with a raw generous energy that I love about mountaineers. When I told him we had turned back at the base of the Lhotse Face, he suggested I was tired from the previous days of climbing. "No big deal. You can try again tomorrow," he said cheerfully, as he clapped a big friendly hand on my shoulder. I appreciated his encouragement, but I had far less confidence than he apparently had in me.

An Unexpected Ally

During the past weeks Steve had become unpopular with some of the rest of the team. In Base Camp he had used up the solar power playing his private DVDs and had run down the batteries on the satellite phones, so others could not email or use the phone. He kept lists of people whom he would help, if they were in trouble on the mountain and those he would not help. The other day Steve threw a fit about his tent floor at Base Camp being uneven. He ragged on about it, even after Ang Dorje made it more level for him.

Lydia noticed Steve was especially nasty to her and me. "Perhaps he doesn't like strong women," she suggested. However the other women on our team were strong and he seemed fine with them. Maybe I remind him of someone he doesn't like, I thought. Oh, stop! I told myself. It's his problem. I won't let him steal my joy. I tried to ignore him, but it was not easy. With my history of feeling badly treated by men, he pushed my buttons. He and I had not spoken to each other for weeks in a tacit pact of mutual dislike.

While the rest of us had climbed to Camp 2, Steve had stayed in Base Camp, sick with a gastrointestinal bug. According to rumors, he was leaving the expedition. Some of us at Camp 2 felt a sense of relief, even a sense of celebration. Then we heard Steve was climbing up to Camp 2 after all. My heart sank. Now I would have to climb the Lhotse Face and share a tent at Camp 3 with someone who hated me. Wonderful, I thought sourly.

I realized that I could not climb the mountain with Steve without talking with him. Find a way to make it work, I coached myself. Find something to like about the guy. I had to admit I admired his persistence. Being sick in the mountains is not for the faint hearted. Later in the afternoon, Steve arrived in Camp. I told myself, the ball is in your court. I walked over to him and said, "I hear you've been really sick. I admire your persistence. How are you now?" "Yeah, it was tough, worse than cancer." he replied. "How are you?"

This was the first time Steve had asked me about myself. Caught off guard, my reply poured out uncensored. "Terrible. I got hypothermia yesterday. Today I tried to climb to Camp 3 and turned back. I have two strikes against me. I probably have lost my chance for a spot on the summit team." Why did I say that, to him of all people? Steve replied, "That's not a useful way to think. It is what it is." At first I bristled. Who was he to lecture me? Then I realized he was right. Wisdom sometimes comes from unexpected sources, even from those we perceive to be our enemies.

Mike radioed to Base Camp to consult Simon about a short-acting asthma inhalant for me. Hedd-wyn had responded well to asthma medications after his breathing troubles a few days ago. Mike and Simon hoped these medications would help me. Weeks ago, when I caught a cold, Simon had me start a long-acting inhalant to prevent asthma, but it did not improve my breathing. Now at Camp 2, Simon suggested adding short-acting asthma medication. New medications make me nervous, as I have a history of atypical reactions. However, I wanted to breathe better.

We set up a medication trial at Camp 2. Mike took my resting pulse and oxygen saturation readings. Then he had me walk briskly -- more of a stumble through the rocks and ice in my big mountaineering boots -- for about 10 minutes around Camp 2. Mike took another set of readings. Then I used the short-acting asthma medication. Thirty minutes later, Mike took more readings, first at rest and then after another stumble around camp. The readings showed no change. I felt just as short of breath. I was disappointed but not surprised.

As I organized my gear for tomorrow's climb, I tried to picture myself, breathing evenly, climbing steadily, and arriving at Camp 3. When anxiety and doubt arose, I firmly told them to leave. I did not sleep much, but I came to peace with myself that night. I would do my best. That was all I could do. Whether I would get a chance for the summit was out of my hands. Worrying about it would not help.

May 14. It was 5:30 am and time to get ready to climb. Instead of sleeping tonight at Camp 3, the plan had changed. Tendi, Lydia, Steve, and I were to climb to Lower or Middle Camp 3 then return to Camp 2 to sleep tonight. Then we could return to Base Camp tomorrow with the rest of our team members. I felt relieved that I did not have to climb all the way to Upper Camp 3 and sleep there, but I was disappointed to miss an important acclimatization experience. I hoped I would be acclimatized well enough without a night at Camp 3, if I got to try for the summit.

Tendi and I left Camp 2 at 6:30 am, ahead of Lydia and Steve, who soon passed us. Steve and I exchanged words of encouragement. This new interaction with Steve was a little disorienting but welcome. Tendi and I arrived at the base of the Lhotse Face in just over two hours. I could see Lydia and Steve climbing the Face just above us. The ice was more scoured and looked scarier than two days ago, when I climbed a little way up using the fixed lines. However, the wind was less fierce today than yesterday, a good thing.

I can do this, I chanted doggedly to myself, talking back to my fear. I jumped the last crevasse, clipped onto the fixed line, and dug my crampons into the Face. I found a rhythm: slide my ascender up the fixed line, place one foot, weight it, take three breaths, slide my ascender up, place the other foot, weight it, take three breaths. I was slow, but my climbing was steady and solid with no slips or falls. Higher up the Face I needed to take as many as 10 breaths per step. Even so, I passed a few very tired climbers with the empty eyes of the completely exhausted. Occasionally, we found a less steep place where other climbers could pass us and where we could take a brief rest to eat and drink a little. Each short rest felt like a tiny piece of heaven, a respite from the chest-heaving work of climbing above 22,000 feet and keeping my fear from careening out of control. I even found energy to chat and joke with climbers with other groups.

After what felt like many hours of climbing, I could see the Yellow Band. This distinctive yellowish layer of rock jutted through the snow and ice above and beyond Camp 3. Then I saw the tents of Lower Camp 3. My heart soared. I'm doing this! I can keep climbing to Middle Camp 3, even Upper Camp 3. I could sleep up there, no problem, my inner optimist chattered, giddy with joy. Lydia and Steve came down to us, as we were climbing beyond Lower Camp 3. We exchanged mutual congratulations. "Hey, let's keep climbing," I suggested eagerly. Lydia replied, "We all should go back to Camp 2 together for safety reasons." I was so glad to have climbed this far and to have felt this good, I nodded agreeably.

To climb down, I had to look down, which exacerbated my fear of heights, especially when I looked down nearly 2,000 feet of this steep hard ice. We could not use our ascenders on the fixed lines, only our safeties. In theory, if I fell, my safety would stop me at the next piece of protection. However that still could be a long way to fall. I would not be the first to die from falling down the Lhotse Face. I grimaced, trying to literally squeeze these terrifying thoughts out of my mind.

As we started down the Face, my fear of heights demons reared their ugly heads. I assumed a tense exaggerated stance with bent knees, like sitting in an imaginary chair, as I had been taught by American Alpine Institute guides for descending icy slopes like this. My quads burned like fire. Lydia shouted at me to relax and go faster. When I tried to relax and speed up, she shouted at me when my footwork got sloppy. My tense climbing was exhausting, but sooner than I could have hoped, we reached the bottom of the Face. I had done it! I had climbed to Camp 3 and back and survived!

We cruised back to Camp 2. The rest of our team greeted us like long lost relatives. Even Steve gave me an awkward pat of congratulations on my shoulder. Our transformation from enemies to allies seemed like a miracle. When Mike radioed our friends at Base Camp to report our progress, I howled "AAAHHHOOOO!!!", brimming with triumph. A thin crackly howl came over the radio in reply. I threw back my head and laughed with happy abandon.

May 15. Today we would head back to Base Camp. As I prepared for today's climb down through the Icefall, a cheery chant floated through my head. Thicker air! Warmer temperatures! Showers! Clean clothes! Chhongba's fabulous meals! What a wonderful day!

Tendi and I cruised down to Camp 1 in about an hour. Once we were in the Icefall, we would not have many chances to stop. In preparation I visited the toilet crevasse and stripped off a layer of clothing. At my tent, I dropped off my mug, bowl, spoon, some warm layers of clothing, and other things I would need for the summit climb, if I were selected for the summit team. I slathered my face with sunscreen, adjusted my glacier goggles and gloves, and checked my climbing harness and crampons. It was Icefall time.

My team mates already had started climbing down the Khumbu Icefall. I could see them below me, bobbing in and out of sight through the maze of fallen seracs and crevasses. I felt good about my climbing, until I got to the Ladder Bridge From Hell. Today it sloped downward and slanted sideways at a weird angle, as though it wanted to tip anyone crossing it into the huge crevasse it spanned. Tendi crossed easily. Then I followed.

I chanted my way onto the Ladder Bridge From Hell, "om mani padme hoom, om mani padme hoom…" The bridge shivered like a horse trying to shed a biting fly, then wobbled and bounced more violently. About three quarters of the way across, one of my crampons got stuck in the rungs. My usual trick of shifting my weight back to free it did not work. The wobbling intensified. I nearly puked in terror. Steady, I ordered myself, throwing up and shaking knees are not allowed right now. I squatted low and eased my butt down onto the ladder, so I could use my hands to free my trapped foot. That did not work. I tried to stand back up, but my pack dragged me backwards. My center of gravity was too far behind my feet. My bulky mountaineering boots prevented me from getting my weight up and over my feet again.

A sense of panic began to overwhelm me. My breaths came in frightened little gasps. Tendi impassively came back onto the ladder bridge and freed my trapped foot. Shaking like a leaf in high wind, I scooted the rest of the way across the wobbly ladder on my butt, feet, and hands. "Thanks," I murmured. I was grateful for Tendi's help, but I felt humiliated. I was as helpless as a child without him.

We climbed down through the rest of the Icefall without further incident. Ang Tsering and Simon met us in Lower Lake Lands with bottles of Sprite, big smiles and hugs. We finished our sodas and traded news. In Base Camp, more hugs and congratulations came from team mates and camp staff. It was good to be home. I looked forward to a few days of the familiar Base Camp routines of eating well, taking a shower, doing hand laundry, emailing, reading, writing in my journal, and chatting with my team mates.

After dinner, I settled into my sleeping bag, trying to avoid new lumps and hollows the shifting glacier had made under my tent. Without warning I vomited twice into my pee bowl, which was fortunately empty and clean. "Are you sick, Carol?" I heard Lydia ask from her tent next door. "I don't think so. I think it's a one off." I replied, trying to sound reassuring. Lydia answered, "Call me if you have another one off." Lydia's concern was touching and reassuring. Advice from my Cho Oyu team mate, Chuck McGibbon, flashed through my mind, "Don't get sick; don't give the guides a reason to turn you back." I must not get sick now that we were so close to our summit climb.

Gummi Bears From Laurel

May 16. I woke up to a tent interior sparkling with frost. After last night's tricky tummy, I went to the mess tent and ate a light breakfast cautiously. It stayed down. Laurel presented me with a zip lock bag of Gummi Bears with "Summit Gummi's for Carol, you can do it! ☺" written on it. She had remembered that I could not find any before our last climb. Her encouragement deeply moved me, especially since my chances for being chosen for the summit team seemed poor.

Today Simon would give each of us a physical exam. We had been living above 17,600 feet for over a month. Living and climbing at high altitude is necessary for acclimatization, but it can take a heavy toll on the body. I was curious – and nervous –about what Simon would find. Dressed in my cleanest glacier pants, I went to the medical tent. Simon measured my blood pressure. It was 140 over 80, higher than my usual 110 over 60. Simon reassured me that elevated blood pressure was not unusual for climbers living at high elevation. My resting heart rate was 68 beats per minute, also higher than its usual 38 to 42. My oxygen saturation was 85%. At home, this reading would have sent me to the Emergency Department, but here it was normal. Simon listened to my lungs. He said the sounds he heard were consistent with scarring from past bouts of pneumonia. Just in case I had an infection, he gave me three days of antibiotics and some medicated throat lozenges.

Next I met with the guides for a "summit briefing." I imagined it to be like a job interview for a spot on the summit team. I was sure they would say, "Nice effort, but it's not enough. You are too slow." I entered the guide tent and sat nervously in a plastic chair across from the guides. My heart thudded in my chest like a jack hammer. I hoped they would not recheck my heart rate and blood pressure now. To ease my nervousness, I joked, "You must have liked my resume well enough to invite me to this job interview." They looked a bit puzzled then smiled wanly, which did not seem promising. I braced myself for bad news.

The guides started with the results of Simon's physical exam. To my surprise, they said that my oxygen saturation and heart rate were similar to those of the other team members and even some of the Sherpas. Mike added that I had trained hard before the expedition and had taken more acclimatization walks during the expedition than the other team members. He and Simon had talked about my problems with shortness of breath. Though it was usually against Adventure Consultants' policy, they agreed to let me start supplemental oxygen at Camp 2, a day earlier than usual.

This option was completely unexpected. When I had emailed Adventure Consultants before I even applied to become a member of this expedition, I had asked whether I could start supplemental oxygen early. The answer was an emphatic no. Now the guides were grinning and welcoming me as a member of the summit team! What an unexpected gift! Suddenly the guide tent was too small to contain my happiness. I wanted to shout, leap, and howl with joy. I had a chance for the summit!

I left the guide tent feeling as light as the cold bright air. I noticed Lhakpa and Tendi releveling Phil's tent site. Phil and Hedd-wyn were helping to find rocks to fill the bigger hollows. Bursting with elation, I eagerly joined them, carrying rocks and stomping the tent site level. Tendi offered to level my tent. I suggested that we level Lydia's before mine, as she had complained about her uneven bed this morning. "I look after you," Tendi said. "Yes, you do," I answered, "Thanks. I appreciate it. But Lydia's tent is worse than mine. We'll do mine if we have time." We leveled Lydia's tent site then started on mine. We were part way done, when Victor came by and invited me to join him and some of the others for bouldering near Pumori Base Camp. I had had such a nice time bouldering with the guys near Pheriche, I really wanted to go. I asked Tendi whether he minded if I joined them. He said OK, but I sensed he was annoyed. Only now, as I write this, do I realize Tendi probably felt tricked into doing more work than his job description specified. That was not my intention.

This time Victor brought a couple of climbing harnesses and a rope so we could belay each other on some of the taller boulders. Full of high spirits, Hedd-wyn immediately jumped onto a boulder and climbed up about 15 feet. Victor scolded him for climbing without a belay. Now was not the time to fall and break an ankle, just before we would start our final climb to Everest's summit. Cheryl, Nikki, Phil, Hedd-wyn, Victor, and I took turns belaying each other. We encouraged each other and cheered, when someone made an especially bold move. We played with childlike abandon in the thin sunshine.

May 17. I woke to birds singing, a new experience in Base Camp. My spirit soared with their melodious notes. Spring was climbing up the mountain. Lydia was singing a cheery little song in her tent next door. I loved our tent village. I would miss it, when this expedition was over. Summit! Summit! I have a chance for the summit! sang a happy little chant inside my head, as I dressed.

A thin streamer of clouds lingered midway up the snow-fluted mountains behind my tent. I sat on a boulder in the sun and watched Base Camp wake up. We ate a leisurely rest day breakfast sitting in plastic chairs in the sunshine. Our climbing Sherpas returned from supplying our high camps. As they strode through Base Camp, we gave them a standing ovation. As usual, they ducked their heads and grinned shyly. These guys were the real heroes. They risked their lives preparing the route, establishing high camps, and stocking them with supplies, so we could have our adventure, our climb of a lifetime, a goal that probably mystified many of them.

Later in the morning, we met in the mess tent for a briefing about our oxygen equipment. We could choose either a Poisk mask, which I had used on Cho Oyu, or a newer TopOut mask, which reputedly delivered oxygen more efficiently than other designs. I took a TopOut mask from the pile on the dining table, put it on, and adjusted it to fit around my goggles and balaclava. It was less bulky and lighter than the Poisk mask, which I liked.

Next we practiced attaching our regulator to a cylinder of compressed oxygen. Though I had worked with compressed gases in my work as a research chemist years ago, the sudden loud hiss of escaping gas was still alarming. We reviewed how to remove ice from the frozen moisture in our breath without damaging the mask. We learned how to be sure oxygen was flowing from the regulator into the mask. We practiced assembling the equipment and placing our in-use oxygen cylinder in the left side of our pack, a spare cylinder in the right side, then putting on the pack and mask without getting tangled in hoses and straps.

From now on, we would be responsible for caring for this equipment. If we damaged it, our chances for a safe summit and return would not be good. I carefully wrapped my mask and regulator in bubble wrap and took them to my sleeping tent. Then I made a list of things to do before our last climb up the mountain: shower, bring in my drying hand laundry before the afternoon snow squalls started, sew buttons back on my glacier shirt, email the folks back home, recharge my digital camera's batteries, pack meds and snacks for ten days higher on the mountain. I did not want to forget anything that might help me reach the summit.

Some of us took a break from our summit preparations and watched the DVD, "World's Fastest Indian." It was the story of an aging New Zealander, who took his old-fashioned motorcycle to the Bonneville Salt Flats and, against the odds, set a world speed record. It was the perfect movie for me to see before I tried to summit Everest, also against the odds.

Waiting for Weather

May 18. At 3:30 am, I woke to the familiar hiss of stoves in the kitchen tent and the scent of burning juniper at the puja altar. For several days we had restlessly watched other expeditions head up the mountain for their summit attempt. Today was our turn.

I was excited yet scared, wavering between confidence and doubt. I reminded myself that even very experienced mountaineers had written about similar roller-coaster emotions. I chanted Mike's mantra to myself: think about what you need to do in the next five minutes and the next hour, don't worry about summit. I began a practiced routine of getting ready while avoiding my frosty tent walls. Even after weeks on this mountain, I still did not like the shower of frost, when the tent walls were disturbed.

We moved through the lower part of the Khumbu Icefall in the predawn half light, Simon and Mark flanking us, swept along by the collective thrill of our summit climb. As the sky lightened, Mark filmed Cheryl and Nikki. Our hushed voices could not conceal a palpable electricity of excitement. This was the real deal, our summit climb.

The Icefall had changed, since we had climbed through it a few days ago. In Lower Lake Lands, some of the frozen lakes were now thawed, so the route was longer, snaking around the open water between the ice ridges. Higher in the Icefall the longer warmer days had collapsed seracs, opened new crevasses, and caused avalanches, burying sections of the fixed lines. Some old ladder bridges were gone, and new ones had been added. Parts of the route, so familiar a few days ago, were now unrecognizable.

As I crossed each ladder bridge, I mentally checked it off to give myself a sense of progress. High in the Popcorn, I faced my nemesis, The Ladder Bridge From Hell. Though was now more steeply angled upward, it did not slope sideways as much as last time, when I got stuck and Tendi freed my boot. I chanted my way across, "om mani padme hoom." I was relieved to get across this time without a fuss.

As usual, the last hour to Camp 2 was slow for me. Climbing into and out of the three large crevasses at the start of the Western Cwm was no easier than previous times. I arrived in camp last, just after Cheryl and Nikki, in about six hours. I was carrying more in my pack than previous climbs, but my slowness disappointed me. I had hoped to be stronger and faster by now. For the thousandth time, I silenced my inner critic. I had gotten here. That was what counted.

My team mates and I stowed our ice axe, crampons, and hiking poles outside our sleeping tents, took off our harnesses and lounged on our Z-rests in the intermittent sunshine. As the clouds sailed overhead, we lobbed snowballs at each other. Ang Dorje nailed me with a big one. I threw badly, so I sneaked up on him and stuffed a big handful of snow down his back. Victor scolded me for being mean. I could not tell whether he was serious or teasing. When I tried to make amends by scooping some of the snow from inside Ang Dorje's jacket, I realized how this could look and joked about making his wife jealous.

After lunch, I could hear a lively card game in one of the two-person sleeping tents. I was not much of a card player and usually preferred to read or write in my journal. Today I wanted to be with my team mates. I found the card players and asked whether there was room for one more. I stared through the tent's entrance at the impossible tangle of seven people's arms, legs, and bodies inside and started to turn away. Someone said, "Sure, come on in."

Somehow we found room. I wove my legs under Lydia's and over Mike's. I did not know the rules to the game, but the others patiently taught me. Everyone won a few games, even me. Eventually we untangled our stiff legs, eased our aching backs, and stumbled back to our own sleeping tents. I glowed with a warm sense of belonging.

May 19. The climb up the Western Cwm to Camp 2 was easier today than previous times. My crampons squeaked, as they bit cold hard ice. I found a steady slow rhythm of two breaths per step. As the sun rose over the surrounding peaks, the Cwm became very hot. I peeled off a jacket to keep from overheating. Climbing up the last hated gulch of expedition trash, rock, and ice was as tedious as ever. At last we reached our tents in Camp 2.

During lunch, Mike briefed us about our schedule for the next few days. Weather data, radioed to Mike from Base Camp, indicated increasing humidity and higher winds, a recipe for a dangerous storm higher on the mountain. We would wait a couple days in Camp 2 and hope for better conditions before we moved up to Camp 3.

Now that we had begun our summit climb, waiting was difficult. I did not see much of my team mates. Perhaps like me, they were taking time to get their heads around our summit climb, along with the hard work and risks involved. Camp 2 was not a fun place to wait. It lacked the teeming excitement of Base Camp and the pristine white snow and ice of Camp 1. Heaps of rock, dirty ice, and crevasses made getting around tricky. Surrounded by high mountain ridges, the sun reached Camp 2 late and left early. After dark we coughed through the night, sounding like a colony of barking seals. Sleep was elusive.

Time slowed to a crawl. Inside my tent I rechecked my gear, going over again and again what I would take higher on the mountain and what I would leave behind. Should I bring 'fox food,' which works well for me in the Icefall, or rely on GU (a high energy gel with electrolytes) and Gummi Bears only? Should I bring a book to read in case we were delayed higher on the mountain? Lots of tent time without a good book can be murder. I did not want to carry unnecessary weight, but I did not want to forget something essential. When I felt overwhelmed or discouraged, I fingered the zip lock bag of Gummi Bears Laurel had given me at Base Camp and reread what she had written on it, "Summit Gummi's for Carol, you can do it! ☺".

When I could not stand being in my tent any longer, I took short walks. Reverting to a childhood hobby, I looked for sparkly rocks in the moraine, pausing occasionally to look up and study the sky. Spindrift billowed from the spectacular jagged ridge of rock and snow between Everest and its neighboring peak, Lhotse, evidence of the high winds Mike wanted to avoid. I felt sorry for anyone who was up there now. Seeing the blowing spindrift made waiting a little easier, but I still worried that the weather would deteriorate further, nixing our climb for the summit. When doubt bubbled up through my mind like toxic waste, I told myself Mike had made the right decision to wait.

Back inside my tent, I read or wrote in my journal. At sunset Zangbu called "Dinner ready!" I moaned to myself, oh, God, now I have to make myself eat. Then I remembered what Guy Cotter had said about setting specific goals for eating enough. I stretched, took my pre-dinner medications, crawled out of my sleeping bag and into a couple of jackets, pulled my outer boots on over my down booties, and shuffled downhill through rocks and ice to the mess tent. Tonight it took me half an hour to eat a half cup of mashed potatoes in tiny slow bites. The potatoes stayed down, a small victory. Now if I could just get some sleep between my own coughing jags and those of my neighbors....

Dig Deep

May 22. At breakfast, Mike said we would climb to Camp 3 today. Suddenly time sped up. So much to do! Hastily I stuffed my huge minus 40 degree down sleeping bag into its compression sack and paused to catch my breath before squeezing the air out of my Thermarest and folding my Z-rest. Even the smallest tasks were tiring, but I was too excited to notice much. At the last minute I took a book out of my pack and kept a single spare pair of liner gloves and a set of brand new socks for the summit climb.

In the mess tent, I ate a cautious breakfast. As I said goodbye to Zangbu and started to leave, Passang came running after me, his eyes round with concern. He was holding my climbing harness, which I had left in the mess tent. I felt stupid about forgetting it after all these weeks on the mountain. With harness and crampons on and supplemental oxygen flowing at one liter per minute, Tendi and I left Camp 2 and climbed toward the Lhotse Face.

The low rate of supplemental oxygen transformed the now-familiar climb to the base of the Lhotse Face. During my previous three climbs, every step had been torture. I had felt weak and starved for oxygen. Now my progress was less labored and even joyful. "Hi, how are you doing?" I chirped cheerfully to climbers with other expeditions. A happy little chant sang inside my head, Climbing this mountain, going for the summit!

As we approached the Lhotse Face, I noticed three people ahead sitting just before the climb gets steeper, taking a rest. Suddenly one of their climbing helmets skittered down the icy slope, gaining speed then leaping toward the big crevasses below. One of the three climbers got up and carefully picked his way down to retrieve the helmet. Then a water bottle hurtled down the same slope. Someone was having a bad day. The falling helmet and water bottle reminded me how quickly gear – and people – can gain speed when falling.

Tendi and I jumped the last crevasse and clipped onto the fixed line for the steep icy climb up the Lhotse Face. I increased my oxygen flow rate to two liters per minute. As we inched upwards, the route now felt more familiar and less frightening. Climber traffic had created more distinct steps in the ice, so it was easier to jab in more crampon points without having to roll my ankles into awkward positions. I flared my boot toes into a wide duck foot gait, made every foot placement solid, and front pointed on steeper sections.

About every hour or so, Tendi and I found a relatively safe place out of other climbers' way and took a short break. I found a stable stance, carefully took off my pack and clipped it to an unused fixed line. We sat on our packs for a few minutes, while we went through our self care tasks. I was the only climber using supplemental oxygen today. I ignored stares from others and resisted my inner critic's whispered poison, you are too slow, you are too weak. A happy descant drowned out my negative self-talk. I was so happy to be here, headed for the summit!

Sooner than I expected, we were climbing past Lower Camp 3. Now we were in unknown territory, higher than I had climbed on Everest. Anxious butterflies fluttered in my belly. Cheryl, who had climbed to Upper Camp 3 on our previous acclimatization cycle, had described some of these pitches as very steep and exhausting. If she had trouble, would I? Ignoring the butterflies, I focused on taking one step at a time. I was keeping up with the rest of the team today, which was good, I told myself.

Tendi and I inched past Middle Camp 3. I was tired and would have liked to stop here. However, our tents were in Upper Camp 3, which Cheryl said had taken her another hour. Dig deep, I coached myself, you have been more tired on other climbs. You're climbing Everest! You can do this!

Slowly, we crept up a series of snowy shelves in the Face where yellow, orange, and red tents sat like huge inverted tea cups on shelves in a giant cupboard. Our tents were on the highest shelf. We had to unclip from the fixed line, traverse perhaps 50 yards, and scramble up onto our shelf. Focus, I told myself, don't fall now after all the hard work of getting up here. Tendi pointed to the tent he and I would share tonight.

While I took off my crampons and stowed them with my ice axe outside the tent, Tendi filled a pot with clean snow to melt for hot drinks and dinner. I offered to help. "I look after you, Carol Didi," he replied. "Thanks, Tendi Bai. I cook for myself at home. It's nice to have someone cook for me for a change." I turned off my oxygen regulator, pulled my sleeping pads and sleeping bag out of my pack, and made a place to rest near the back of the tent, so Tendi had room to tend our stove at the tent's opening. As he lit the stove under a pot of snow, I added a little water from my water bottle. "Now the snow won't scorch," I explained, "water will taste better." Tendi nodded agreeably as though humoring a crazy person.

We dug through a bag of packaged food and chose what we wanted to eat. I settled on a heat-and-eat pouch of beans and cubed ham. Tendi chose a similar pouch of pale sausages. We added them to the pot of melting snow to heat. While Tendi tended the stove, Sherpas from other expeditions stopped at the entrance of our tent, sat on their heels, and chatted, as Tendi filled their mugs with hot tea. I busied myself by rolling up food packaging, making it compact and easy to carry off the mountain during our descent.

Between visits from other Sherpas, I asked Tendi about his family. Tendi was from a village near Lukla. One of ten children, he was 38 years of age. He looked younger with his compact body and smooth brown face. One of his brothers lived in Japan and another in Austria. Tendi had visited his brother in Austria. A younger brother and sister were in college in Kathmandu. The brother was studying business and banking. The sister was studying water management. Other siblings lived in his home village, farming and herding dzos.

Tendi has four children. I asked whether his marriage had been arranged or was a love match. "A little of both," he answered with a shy smile. Tendi's eldest child, a son of 15, wanted to be a climbing Sherpa, Tendi told me with obvious pride. His daughter, age 13, did not know what she wanted to do yet. Tendi's two younger sons, age 11 and 9, went to school at a monastery. When they were older they could leave the monastery or stay and train to be monks. Tendi said he wanted Sherpa kids to think being Sherpa was cool. I nodded in agreement. Sherpas are known for their strength and dependability, qualities valued across cultures.

When Tendi was not working as a climbing Sherpa, he worked on his farm. He mulched with grass, as I did in my vegetable garden at home. Tendi used to have dzos, but they were expensive and too much trouble. I nodded with empathy. I used to have horses. As much as I loved them, they were expensive and made getting away for trips difficult. I was delighted to find that Tendi and I had several things in common, even though we lived on opposite sides of the world in very different cultures.

I asked Tendi what he would do, if he could do whatever he liked. His brow furrowed in puzzlement. I had to ask the question several times, before he understood. "Nothing," he said finally. "You want to do nothing?" I asked, not sure I had understood. "Yes," he replied, grinning broadly. Perhaps Tendi's life was so strenuous and dangerous, that doing nothing seemed like a well-deserved rest to him. To a driven person like me, the idea of doing nothing was terrifying.

Our pouches of food were hot and ready to eat. I used a crampon point to start a hole in the tough plastic bag, so I could pour the beans and ham into my bowl. Tendi's bowl, full of pale sausages, looked unappetizing, even vaguely obscene. He teasingly insisted I eat one. "Ok, only if you will eat some of my beans," I answered. We giggled like naughty children, as we scraped portions from our own bowls into each other's. To my surprise, the beans and ham tasted really good, the first meal I had enjoyed, since we left Base Camp days ago. I wished I had more to eat, but I did not want to risk an attack of the pukes.

After dinner, I was too scared to leave the tent to go to the crevasse toilet. Climbers have slipped and fallen to their deaths on the Lhotse Face, often on their way to the toilet. I waited until Tendi seemed to be asleep and used my pee bowl. Then I settled into my sleeping bag for the night. I turned on my regulator to a flow rate of one liter per minute, checked my oxygen line for ice, and put on my mask.

I am a lousy sleeper under the best of circumstances, so I had low expectations for tonight. While wearing my oxygen mask, each breath made a rasping roar. My rational mind knew that wearing the mask provided more oxygen than sleeping without it, but the mask felt like it was suffocating me. When I could not stand it any more, I would take off my mask, turn off my regulator, and lie on my side. Sometimes I could doze for a little while. When lying on my side made my hip hurt, I would turn my oxygen back on, replace my mask, and lie on my back for awhile. I needed to sleep, but I also needed the supplemental oxygen to help me recover from today's climb to Camp 3 and for tomorrow's climb of over 2,000 vertical feet higher to Camp 4. Through the night, I alternated between wearing the mask and taking it off. Best of both worlds, I humored to myself, hoping it was true. Mercifully, the night was calm, with no wind to flap the tent walls. Tendi's snores were soft, like a cat purring. Eventually, I knew I had slept, because I had crazy altitude dreams about being chased through foreign airports by murderous thugs, a classic anxiety dream.

The Death Zone

May 23. Another cold day dawned without storms, a gift from the mountain gods. Good weather had held for so long, it seemed like a miracle. I risked a cautious trip to the crevasse toilet before the others were up. Tendi and I dug through the food bag and found packets of cereal and hot chocolate. I mixed mine together into a muddy mess to save time and ate as much of it as I could. The uneaten portion went into a Zip Lock bag to be carried down the mountain later with the trash. We scoured our bowls with clean snow and packed to leave.

Several other expeditions were also moving up to Camp 4. We paused several times to wait for slower climbers ahead of us. For me slow was good. I could easily keep up with the rest of my team mates. My breathing was deep and steady, and I had time to make sure each foot placement was solid.

Phil Drowley climbing above Camp 3 on the Lhotse Face, May 23, 2008, photo by Mike Roberts.

Our tents at Camp 3 seemed to shrink below us to toy tent size, as we climbed higher. Climbing Sherpas from various expeditions carried heavy packs, passing us on their way up to Camp 4. Other Sherpas were descending to Camp 2. We tried to get out of their way as much as possible. Passing people was tricky and dangerous on the fixed lines, because one person must unclip momentarily. Usually the gallant young Sherpas unclipped and passed me, while I stood still and remained clipped to the fixed line. "No problem," they murmured, as I thanked them.

Climbers bunched at the base of the Yellow Band, one of the usual bottle necks on Everest. As I gazed up the route, I noticed that some sections were quite steep. However, when it was my turn to climb, the eroded yellowish rock provided plenty of hand and foot holds. The challenge was to keep my goggles from frosting over, when I looked down to see where to place my feet. My heart raced on some of the steeper sections, but I climbed without any slips or falls. I felt pleased with myself. Later I learned that one of our other climbers needed a push by a Sherpa on the behind to get up the Yellow Band.

On some of the snowy stretches I noticed two ropes were running between my ascender and the next piece of protection, a puzzling and yet strangely familiar sight. Then I remembered altitude had played this trick on me before on Cho Oyu. One of the "ropes" was the fixed line's shadow on the snow. I was pleased to figure out this little illusion faster than on Cho Oyu.

Above the Yellow Band, a vast jagged ridge of snow, rock, and ice stretched above us between the Geneva Spur on Everest's flank and Lhotse's summit. Pure white snow laced the boldly folded layers of limestone, evidence of the unimaginably powerful forces that continue to lift the world's highest mountains. People ask why I climb. This other worldly beauty is one reason. I felt as though I were in an enchanted dream.

On the Traverse above the Yellow Band with the ridge between Everest and Lhotse in the background, May 23, 2008, photo by Mike Roberts.

Darker thoughts came. In a few hours, we would begin our final climb for the summit. I had not slept much for the past several nights. I worried that we would get into Camp 4 late and not have enough time to rest, eat, and drink before climbing the last 3,000 feet of elevation to the top. Worrying does not help, focus on the next step, the next breath, I reminded myself over and over again. Each time we paused, I focused on self care tasks.

As we began what is known as the Traverse, the steep drop to the left looked a very long way down – and very scary. To counter my fear of heights, I kept my gaze straight ahead on where I needed to place each foot. I concentrated on placing each foot carefully and passing my safety and ascender as efficiently as possible around pieces of protection. Ahead, the Geneva Spur looked steep, intimidating, and very far away. Everest's summit pyramid, with its signature banner cloud of blowing spindrift, loomed in the distance. As we climbed hour after hour, it got closer.

Approaching the Geneva Spur with Everest's summit pyramid and signature banner cloud in the background, May 23, 2008, photo by Mike Roberts.

The Geneva Spur was a mixture of black rock, ice, and snow -- tricky to climb wearing crampons. Some climbers removed their crampons here. However, getting them back on could be tricky while standing on uneven footing with the big drop off on our left. I left mine on. A tangle of many fixed lines, some left from previous seasons, made choosing the safer ones confusing. Old lines caught crampons and tripped some climbers, but I avoided any trips or slips. Once we were climbing it, the Geneva Spur was not as difficult as I had expected. Slowly, we approached its top. When I dared, I looked up and craned my neck, hoping to spot Camp 4.

Finally I saw a tent. Then, as I kept climbing, more tents appeared several hundreds of yards ahead. Do I dare hope we were nearing Camp 4? Yes! We were here! The day's climb was done! The climb to 26,000 feet elevation had been surprisingly easy. I can do this, I can summit Everest. Piece of cake! my inner optimist crowed. My confidence rose like a hot air balloon on a clear calm day.

Camp 4, a scattering of yellow and orange tents, sat on the edge of the South Col, a giant saddle of black rock and wind-swept ice. My gaze swept across the South Col and up Everest's black summit pyramid, laced with snow and ice. Mike came up along side me. "That's where we climb tonight, to the summit," he said, pointing up the massive pyramid. Two tiny figures were climbing up its lower flanks, dwarfed by its vastness. I wondered why they were climbing at this time of day. It was too late to summit today and too early to summit tomorrow. Was there trouble higher on the mountain, and they were going to help?

As I stared up at the towering pyramid, it began to mess with my head. It looked like a very long hard climb. I could not even see the Balcony, where we would make our first stop to change our oxygen cylinders, never mind the route beyond, which was supposed to be even more difficult than what was visible from here. The confidence I had felt only a moment ago shriveled up and blew away. I mumbled something unintelligible in reply to Mike, trying to sound braver than I felt.

Camp 4 sat on the threshold of the Death Zone. Here, the body cannot acclimatize further to the thin air. The digestive system shuts down, the body consumes its own tissues, and begins to die. Few people have survived for more than 48 hours in the Death Zone.

As I gazed across the vast South Col, I could see how the ill-fated climbers of the 1996 tragedy had descended to this vast saddle, became lost in the storm, and could not find their tents. Now, a dozen years later, we picked our way across this broad saddle through jagged rock, snow, ice, broken tent poles, shredded tents, discarded clothing, empty oxygen cylinders, spent fuel canisters, food packaging, and human waste. In recent years some expeditions had made special efforts to remove garbage from past climbs, but Camp 4 was still the trashiest camp I had ever seen. I could understand how climbers could exhaust themselves and not have the energy to carry down their trash, but it was still disgusting and depressing.

I did not want to have to "go" during tonight's climb for the summit, so I set out to try to do the necessary. The South Col provided little privacy. There were no boulders or other features to go behind. Most climbers walked away from the tents toward the lowest part of the Col and swatted in the rocks. There lay what looked like the tent-wrapped body of a young climber who died yesterday. I felt a painful pit of sadness in my belly.

We had heard rumors about the deceased climber. He was a young Swiss man who was attempting to summit all 14 peaks over 8,000 meters without supplemental oxygen. He and his companions had summited Everest, but he had collapsed during their descent. His companions had dragged him from the South Summit to Camp 4, a remarkable feat. They had left him for a few minutes to get medicine. When they had returned, he had died. I wondered whether we would see more dead bodies and how I would react. The possibility filled me with dread.

I tried not to dwell on these dark thoughts and feelings. I passed the tent-wrapped body as respectfully as I could, pausing to namaste, to acknowledge this young man's tragic passing. My eyes suddenly burned with tears, and my throat tightened painfully. I struggled to master my emotions. I walked quite a ways past the tent bundle out of respect, though each step cost me precious energy needed for tonight's climb.

Inside my assigned tent, my tent mates, Ang Dorje and Robyn, greeted me cheerfully. For the past few days, they both had been stronger and faster than I, yet they had never treated me like a second-rate climber. I appreciated their graciousness.

I would have liked to have rested after today's climb, but I needed to prepare for tonight's summit attempt, which we would begin in a few hours. I knew from past experience these simple tasks would be more tiring and take longer than lower on the mountain.

Between drags of supplemental oxygen and slurping down warm drinks, soup, and noodles, I prepared for the climb to the summit. Huddled inside my minus 40 degrees down sleeping bag, I stripped to the skin and hung my damp layers of clothing from today's climb inside our tent to dry. I would need these clothes for the descent back to Base Camp in a couple of days. Though it was minus 10 degrees Fahrenheit and the moisture in my clothes froze soon after I hung them, the ice would sublime overnight in the thin dry air.

Then I dressed for the final climb. I started with a disposable diaper. I had leaked on Cho Oyu above 26,000 feet elevation, an appalling experience, so this time I would be ready for that unpleasant possibility. I cleaned my feet with half-frozen travel wipes and pulled on brand new synthetic liner socks and wool outer socks, smoothing out the wrinkles to avoid blisters on my feet. I put on a clean base layer, a medium-weight fleece balaclava, and an Outdoor Research Saturn suit (a thick stretchy coverall with convenient zippers for doing the necessary.) Over these layers, I pulled on huge down pants, also with convenient zippers, and hiked their suspenders over my shoulders. I squirmed into my climbing harness and cinched it tight. I had to rest frequently, suck oxygen from my mask, and jam my cold hands into bulky gloves to warm them. My big gloves turned ice cold when I was not wearing them, so I opened a pair of chemical hand warmers and put them inside the gloves.

We would find very few places during the summit climb to stop and take off our packs. Most stuff we would need during the climb we would have to wear on our bodies or carry in our pockets. I put an insulated half liter bottle and a half liter thermos of warm water in the inner chest pockets of my down parka. Though Mike had warned that any liquids outside our parkas would freeze, I insulated a liter bottle of warm water and put it in my pack. Snacks, eye wear, sunscreen, and pee funnel went in various pockets in my layers of clothing and inside my pack lid.

Diamox had helped my body adapt to each camp above Base Camp during the past several weeks. However, it also had acted as a diuretic. Having to pee frequently could be problematic, especially since we would not be able to stop very often. Should I take Diamox or not? Trade offs are an inevitable part of high altitude mountaineering. I decided to take half a pill, about 125 milligrams.

More questions buzzed through my head like a swarm of agitated bees. Have my inner boots dried enough from today's climb to put on now? I pulled off a glove and felt inside an inner boot. It was icy cold. Should I use hand warmers to pre-warm my inner boots before I put them on? The hand warmers in my gloves did not seem to be working. I had not experienced serious trouble with cold hands and feet on previous climbs, but others in our group had various hand and feet warming devices. I hoped my hands and feet would be warm enough. Worrying about it won't help, I reminded myself for the millionth time. I pulled on the cold inner boots, shoved my feet back into my sleeping bag, and hoped for the best.

When we thought we were finished with our preparations, Robyn and I would lie down and rest on top of our sleeping bags. Moments later I would remember something else I needed to do, sit up, and get busy again. I was too excited to rest anyway. "Guys, we're doing this!" I said to Robyn and Ang Dorje, as excited as a little kid on Christmas morning. They grinned back at me, eyes sparkling with anticipation.

166

Breath of the Mountain Goddess

At 7:30 pm, it was time to get out of the tent and put on my big red down parka, outer boots, crampons, and pack. I crawled out of the tent like a prehistoric beast, pushing my pack in front of me. It was clear, cold, and dead calm. After struggling into my outer boots, I squinted in the dark at the thermometer on my pack. It read minus 15 degrees Fahrenheit, warm by Everest standards. I felt lucky, even as my face turned numb, and icy night air crept into my gloves and boots. It would get colder, as we climbed through the night.

To take my mind off this chilling thought, I looked up at the night sky. The Milky Way was bigger and brighter than I had ever seen it, like a vast black velvet shawl sparkling with heavenly gems. The bejeweled sky looked unfamiliar, as though I were viewing it from another galaxy. I stared in awe, my senses overloaded with beauty.

During a previous season another Salt Lake climber, Dr. Doug Brockmeyer, had frozen his corneas during a cold windy Everest climb. Before I left home, he had advised me to bring some clear goggles for climbing at night to protect my eyes. I had brought a pair of lacrosse goggles and put them on now. The goggles frosted up. I could not see. I took them off and tried cleaning them, but ice stuck stubbornly to the lenses. My glacier goggles and ski goggles were too dark to see well enough at night. It was dead calm here at Camp 4. I glanced at Tendi, who was not wearing goggles. If he was climbing without eye protection, it must be OK, I reasoned. I tossed the lacrosse goggles back inside my tent.

I felt like the Michelin Tire Man in my bulky down clothes, as I bent over and struggled to put on my crampons. Tendi had pity on me and put them on for me. He helped me shoulder my pack and kept my oxygen hoses from tangling. He pulled my gloves and parka cuffs together so they overlapped to keep out the biting cold. He cinched my parka hood tight around my oxygen mask and face. I felt like a toddler being dressed by a protective parent to play in the snow.

Mike assigned Nima Sherpa to join Tendi and me for tonight's climb. Tall, young, and good looking, Nima greeted me with a pleasant smile and polite handshake. Cheryl teased me about having not just one, but two, handsome young Sherpas in attendance tonight. "Hey, when you've got it, flaunt it," I teased back, my words muffled into unintelligible grunts behind my oxygen mask.

Tendi, Nima, and I were ready to go at little before 8 pm. We cleared our departure with Mike. I set my regulator at a flow rate of four liters per minute, the same rate as the rest of my team mates. My heart danced inside my chest with happy excitement. I felt better now than I had a few days ago lower on the mountain. The weather was good, I felt good, and it was all about to happen. This was what we have been working toward for weeks. This was it, the real deal.

We crossed the wide saddle of the South Col, picking our way through rocks, snow, ice, and trash. As we began to climb the first snowy slope, others passed us. Robyn, Ang Dorje, and their Sherpa climbing partners were first. Then came Mike and Lydia with Heddwyn, Steve, and Phil plus their Sherpas. Next were Victor, Cheryl, and Nikki with more Sherpas. Being passed by everyone in our group was demoralizing, but it was far from the first time. Get over it, I told myself, this is not a race. Remember what they call the last person in the class in medical school at graduation. Doctor.

Climbing at night can be a lonely experience. Though other climbers were moving up the mountain, my world was limited to a small circle of light from my headlamp. I could hear the crunch and squeak of Tendi's and Nima's crampons in the ice, but we spoke only in the abbreviated language of mountaineers, keeping our communication focused on coordinating our climb and conserving our energy.

We followed what looked like drag marks from the young deceased climber being hauled by his companions to Camp 4. Depressing thoughts flooded my mind. Will I collapse? Will someone have to drag me down? Will someone else die during tonight's climb? I shook myself mentally and told myself to focus on climbing. Take a step up, breathe, take another step up. Keep going. Concentrate on placing each foot solidly.

To counter depressing thoughts, I occasionally paused a moment and looked up at the route ahead. A strand of sparkling diamonds snaked up the summit pyramid toward the Balcony, where we would stop briefly to change oxygen cylinders. The diamonds were the head lamps of other climbers. I felt a deep bond with these other adventurers, though most were complete strangers. We all were pushing ourselves to the limit to reach the same goal, the highest place on earth.

A full moon rose, backlighting the wispy spindrift now blowing off the ridge above the Balcony. It looked like the ghostly breath of the Mountain Goddess. It was the most spiritual thing I had ever seen. That moment I understood with every fiber of my being why some people believe Everest is sacred, even a goddess. The sky brimming with brilliant stars, the sparkling strand of headlamps on the route ahead, and the swirling goddess breath were so beautiful, my eyes filled with tears. I blinked them away and refocused on climbing.

The route became steeper. We clipped our safeties and ascenders onto fixed lines. Old fixed lines from previous seasons mingled with this season's. Nima and Tendi pointed out this season's safer rope and checked that I had clipped onto it correctly. I appreciated this, as I sometimes had trouble distinguishing new ropes from the old ones and occasionally did not reclip my safety properly in the dark. Nima was particularly helpful and kind. Perhaps helping a Westerner was a novel experience for him, while Tendi seemed a bit blasé after climbing with me for the past several weeks.

The climbing was slow and felt relentlessly up. When my inner whiner started to whimper, I teased myself, Silly SilverFox, of course it's relentlessly up. Everest is the highest mountain in the world! My spirit was really excited about going for the summit, in contrast to my body, which felt slow and not quite with the program. The contrast was weird but no weirder than anything I had experienced before in the mountains.

My right hand prickled uncomfortably. These sensations were worrisome, but pain told me that my hand was not frozen. My hand felt no worse than on previous cold climbs I had done. Later, I realized the prickling was probably side effects from Diamox. Eventually it stopped and was replaced by a more urgent problem.

I had to pee really badly. I asked the Sherpas for a break. Tendi insisted we keep climbing. The situation became critical. I asked again. Again, Tendi insisted we keep going. Nuts! I could not wait any longer. I began to leak. Yuck! At least I was wearing a diaper. When Tendi did finally let me stop to pee, I could not find where I had stashed my pee funnel. Bugger! Oh, well, the damage is already done, I told myself, but I still felt disgusting and embarrassed. Get over it, I growled to myself. It's not the end of the world. Some extreme athletes "go" on the run.

We stopped some time later at a ledge of dark rock at the base of a cliff. We unclipped from the fixed lines and traversed to our left along the ledge to get off the route. This time I found my pee funnel. Facing up the mountain in the dark, I accidentally peed on my ascender, which was hanging by its leash from my harness. I had forgotten to clip it up properly. The ascender became instantly encased in a glassy shell of frozen urine. Rats! I can't do anything right tonight, even after weeks of using this equipment, I growled to myself. I tried tapping the ascender on the rocky cliff to shatter the ice. No joy. Fortunately the ascender still worked. The frozen pee sublimed from ice to vapor during the next hour. I was thankful Everest had forgiven me for this stupid mistake.

On we climbed, hour after hour. I must be lost in some strange endless loop, destined to climb forever, I thought wearily. A few climbers were already climbing down. They had the blank stares and stumbling gaits of the half dead. Because it was still very dark and too early for them to have summited, I suspected they had given their all and not summited. I felt bad for them. I wondered whether I too would turn back without summiting.

Turn Back

I struggled up an especially steep pitch of jagged black rock, leaning backwards on the fixed line to find foot holds and hand holds. The fixed lines provided some protection from a serious fall and partially numbed my terror, but I still hated leaning backwards. The pitch was not technically difficult, but it was clumsy in big gloves, an oxygen mask that pushed up into my eyes every time I looked down at my feet, a huge down parka, fat down pants, and bulky three-layer boots with crampons. At over 26,000 feet elevation, I felt as though I were climbing against Jovian gravity in a space suit. Each cycle of movements took every ounce of will I had: look for a foot hold, bend my knee and lift my foot up onto the hold, test it, shift my weight over it, straighten my knee, slide my ascender up the fixed line, repeat this cycle again and again and again.

At the top of this steep pitch, I paused on my hands and knees, my breath coming in sharp ragged gasps, which triggered violent coughing. I coughed so hard I expected to spit up bits of lung tissue. I fought to get enough air.

My inner critic hissed poisonously, if you are having this much trouble now, before we have even reached the Balcony, you should turn back now. If you collapse and cannot climb on your own, you put Nima and Tendi in added danger. You vowed not to endanger anyone else unnecessarily. Slowly, I stood up and tried to steady my ragged breathing. Tendi asked, "Carol Didi, you OK?" I was too out of breath to answer. He leaned forward and pressed his forehead to mine, a gentle Sherpa gesture of affection and respect. We stood that way for what seemed like a very long time, but it was probably only for a few seconds. My jangled nerves and uneven breathing steadied. Tendi and I parted. "I'm OK, Tendi Bai," I heard myself say. I took a couple of slow centering breaths. "Let's go." The firmness and resolve in my voice surprised me. It was as though a stronger more confident me were speaking, not the me who seriously considered turning back.

After perhaps another hour of climbing -- high altitude plays tricks on my ability to estimate the passage of time -- we came to the first relatively un-steep spot, since we had left the South Col. "Sit here, Carol Didi," Tendi said. I took off my pack and sat against a rock that poked into my back and butt uncomfortably, too tired to shift away from the pointy rocks. After several hours of climbing, I was grateful to sit down.

Suddenly wind whipped needles of ice into my eyes. I yelped and covered my face with my gloved hands. I asked for help getting my ski goggles from my pack lid, as I could not see. The Sherpas did not respond. My eyes burned, and my eyelashes started to freeze together. I tried to claw the ice from my eyes with fat gloved fingers, which did not work. I tried taking off a thick outer glove, but intense cold stiffened my hand into a useless paw. I was afraid the sharp wind would rip my glove from its leash around my wrist. A lost glove meant I would lose my hand to frostbite. I managed to get the glove, whipping in the wind from its leash, back on my very cold hand. I alternated between squeezing my eyes shut and squinting to see through icy eyelashes.

I heard the hollow clang of metal. Tendi and Nima must have been changing our oxygen cylinders. Slowly it came to me: we must be at the Balcony. Then we have been climbing for at least four hours. My spirits soared. This was the first evidence of our progress toward the summit

Tendi said it was time to go. Again I asked for help finding my goggles, but he turned away and started climbing. As we inched up an exposed rocky ridge, the wind blasted my eyes repeatedly. I squinted to shield them as best as I could. As I staggered up the ridge, I grabbed the right edge of my parka's hood and pulled it down to protect my eyes from the wind-driven ice crystals. Every time I passed a piece of protection on the fixed line, I needed both gloved hands to remove and reattach my safety and ascender. Each time I let go of my hood, it blew off my head, and my eyes received another painful blast. The windward side of my face felt flash frozen. Gusts of wind jostled me, like malevolent spirits trying to shove me off the ridge and into the void. I felt as insignificant as an ant crawling up the Empire State Building. Step by step, I inched up the ridge, fighting the wind and the stinging ice crystals.

During lulls in the wind, I would pause, lift my head and peer through my frozen eye lashes. We were now above a vast sea of billowing cumulus clouds that stretched below us as far as I could see. Distant lightning lit up giant cauliflower-like domes of clouds below us, so they glowed like Japanese lanterns in shades of yellow, orange, blue, and green. This surreal light show was completely silent, except for the crunch of our crampons on ice and the whoosh of our breath through our oxygen masks. The lightning was too far away for us to hear even a murmur of thunder. It was eerie and awe inspiring, like nothing I had ever seen. Such beauty made me feel immeasurably rich and fortunate.

I had prepared myself physically and psychologically for a very long cold dark climb before sunrise. Sooner than I expected, a thin band of orange appeared at the eastern horizon. Dawn was coming! I had always loved this moment, the first sign of daybreak. After sunrise the cold would become less fierce. The prospect of climbing the more difficult parts of the summit climb with better visibility cheered me. My eyes still hurt, but the wind was less vicious now.

My eyes felt no worse than the temporary eye irritation I had already experienced lower on the mountain from intense sun, wind, and dry air.

Several times, as I labored up rugged steep terrain, I smelled frying bacon. For a brief time, I was puzzled. No one would be frying bacon above 27,000 feet elevation. Yet this experience seemed familiar. Slowly, a memory rose through my altitude-fogged mind. I had experienced a similar olfactory hallucination about 15 years ago during another demanding event, a 26-hour 76-mile hike through wild country in central Utah. I'm not losing my mind, I'm just hallucinating, I chuckled to myself.

Tendi, Nima, and I came to a rocky point. The route ahead dipped into a small saddle edged with rocky outcroppings. A steep drop off plunged down on my left. In the predawn light I was startled to see a Western guy sitting in the lee of one of the outcroppings. He slowly looked up, as I approached. He had the dazed look of a guy who had done several hard rounds in a boxing match and had lost. We grunted greetings to each other. I learned later he was a guide with a history of altitude problems. He had sent his client climbers on with climbing Sherpas and was waiting for them to return. I noticed oxygen cylinders near him and more cylinders fanning down into the saddle. Tendi told me to sit. I took off my pack, sat, and drank a little icy water, grimacing from the headache it gave me. Tendi and Nima were changing our oxygen tanks again. Could we be at the South Summit? I gazed up the route and recognized the Knife Edge from Everest documentaries. We ARE at the South Summit!

The Knife Edge is the final climb to the true summit. I was overjoyed to have gotten this far. I felt better than I had expected to feel at this point. For weeks, my thoughts about whether I would summit had swung wildly between extreme optimism and extreme pessimism. Now, with only about two and a half more hours of climbing to the summit, I could make a more rational assessment. I had a reasonable chance, barring anything really stupid or catastrophic. Excitement raced through my body like electricity.

Time Stood Still

In the predawn light, I sized up the Knife Edge. What I could see of it did not look any more difficult than other ridge scrambles I had done. Still, it was intimidating. Steep drops on either side of the Knife Edge plunged thousands of feet. Above 28,000 feet elevation, even with supplemental oxygen, my body and brain were not working as well as usual. We still had to get up the Hillary Step. Could I climb it? Or would I get stuck, blocking other climbers like a cork in a bottle? I tried to swallow the lump of fear swelling in my throat. I pushed the Hillary Step from my mind, as I chanted Mike's mantra: think about what you have to do in the next five minutes, the next hour.

Not long after we started to climb the Knife Edge, I watched Tendi traverse a steeply angled smooth slab of rock. Tendi seemed to sticky-foot effortlessly across the featureless slab. I tried to imitate him. I slipped and fell hard on my right hip and slid off the edge, my legs dangling in space. Not good, I thought dully. My brain was too numb to register as much fear as it normally would, perhaps a good thing under the circumstances. Panic would only worsen my situation. Tendi shouted in alarm. Nima tried to grab my down pants and pull me back up onto the rock. My ascender on the fixed line had stopped my fall, but my struggle back up onto the route cost me precious energy.

We climbed on, scrambling over and past pinnacles of gray rock in the growing dawn light. My fall off the route had unnerved me. No harder than what I have done before, I reminded myself over and over, when my legs shook with terror at the vast drop offs on either side of me. Tendi and Nima watched me protectively, as I scrambled over some of the airier gaps between pinnacles.

As I climbed up and over a boulder, I saw a young Sherpa slumped among the rocks. He slowly looked up, gazed toward me through dull unfocused eyes, and lowered his head again. His face was pale and gray. His body looked small, shrunken, and vulnerable. Tendi gently lifted his chin with a gloved hand and spoke to him in Sherpa. Tendi told Nima and me to continue up the Knife Edge, while he stayed with the young Sherpa.

I felt a surge of annoyance. Tendi was supposed to look after me. Then I burned with shame. That young Sherpa could be in serious trouble, even dying. Tendi was doing the right thing to stop and help him. I climbed on, Nima following. Tendi soon caught up with us. "How is the Sherpa?" I asked. "Sherpa OK," Tendi replied. "Good," I said, relieved. I wanted to know more, but we needed to keep moving and focus on our climbing.

Ahead the route took a pronounced dip into a narrow V-shaped pass then rose abruptly. The pass was clogged with climbers slowly moving up and coming down the abrupt rise amid a crazy tangle of ropes. This must be the Hillary Step. We inched closer to it, carefully passing climbers descending to Camp 4 on the narrow traverse. Then we waited in line for our turn to climb.

I nervously watched, as other climbers moved up the Hillary Step. Though they were slow, none of the ascending climbers seemed to be in trouble. The climbing did not look too difficult. I was relieved. At the base of the Hillary Step, I saw a vaguely familiar face among the descending climbers. We exchanged dull stares. Days later I realized it was Mike Hamill, the guide with whom I had climbed

Aconcagua in early 2007. Then I saw other familiar faces, those of my team mates. Steve was descending with Hedd-wyn, Phil, Mike, and Lydia. Oxygen masks muffled our verbal greetings. Steve passed closest to me. I raised my left gloved hand to exchange a knuckle bash with him. He grunted and gave me a feeble waist-high wave that did not reach my glove. He looked totally exhausted. I felt a surge of empathy. This mountain beats up fit young guys like him as well as old women like me, a strange kind of equal opportunity.

As my team mates climbed down past me, I noticed a small Asian woman part way down the Hillary Step above me. About ten feet from the bottom, she sat facing us, her back pressed against the mountain, legs braced, hands and feet clinging to the rock, her face frozen with fear. She was in a panic freeze. Her climbing partners were trying to encourage her to move down.

Climbers behind me shouted at me to start climbing. Climbers above the panic-frozen woman shouted at me to wait. I could not climb and wait at the same time. I had to do one or the other. The impatient shouts behind me became louder and more insistent. I saw a way to pass the frightened Asian woman without endangering her.

I took a deep breath and shoved my ascender up the fixed line with my left hand. I tuned out my fear and the shouts from other climbers and climbed, focusing on each move. For the first dozen moves, I found good holds on the rock on my left and good places to front point ice or to wedge my right boot into the space where ice had melted away from rock. All was going well. I moved left and up onto a rock face with smaller holds past a web of old fixed lines. My feet became trapped, possibly tangled in old fixed lines below me. The wall I was climbing was so steep I could not see what was holding my feet. I kicked, tentatively at first, trying to get free, then I kicked more vigorously. I felt so helpless! I struggled in wild bursts, pausing to gasp for air. My struggles became feebler. They took a lot of energy at nearly 29,000 feet elevation.

During one of my flailing efforts, my feet suddenly came free. Perhaps I had kicked them free. Perhaps Nima or someone else below me had untangled them. "Thanks," I mumbled dully. I pushed and pulled myself upward, leaning backwards on my ascender to see where to place my feet. Finally I could see over the top of the wall. Almost done! I heaved myself up and over the top of the Hillary Step like a breaching whale, heart pounding. Jubilation! I had climbed the Hillary Step! The hard part of the Knife Edge was done.

I looked up at the route ahead. It undulated upward along a scalloped ridge of white cornices, which looked easy after the Step. I was really going to summit Everest! My chest swelled, as though it would explode with joy.

Lydia Bradey (center) nearing Everest's summit with Makalu in the background, May 24, 2008, photo by Mike Roberts.

Don't get cocky, I reminded myself. Stay focused, or you could still blow it. Getting too far out on a cornice, which could break and take me for a big fall, was a real possibility. I carefully looked for safe footing, placed a foot, eased forward onto it, looked, placed, eased forward, moving slowly as if in a dream. No, I am really awake, I reminded myself happily. This is really happening! I moved forward, my sluggish pace at odds with the carnival of glee running wild through my mind. I bounced between rampant happiness and cautious concentration, mirroring the final ripples of the ridge line to the summit.

Ahead I saw a small group of climbers, looking chubby in their down suits, sitting just below the farthest visible cornice. At first, I thought that can't be the summit. Documentaries show hordes of climbers, waiting for their turn to stand for a few precious moments on top of the world. Then I thought nobody sits in a place like that unless it is the summit. My joy started to career out of control. Gonna do it, gonna summit!!! My heart soared like a rocket headed for outer space.

Suddenly my rocket crashed and burned. I could see a distant dark crag looming above the seated climbers. THAT must be the summit. It would take many more hours to get there. My body suddenly felt very heavy and tired. My glee died. I could not do this. It was too far. I had been climbing for over 10 hours above 26,000 feet elevation. Then I thought this is the day I summit Everest. It will take as long as it takes. I shut out negative thoughts. I found a rhythm: step, breathe, breathe, step, breathe, breathe, look up and make sure I was not too close to the cornice edge, step, breathe, breathe.

We passed one cornice then another and another. The dark distant "summit" crag slowly shrank in height, as I climbed toward it. Weird. Then I realized the altitude was messing with my mind again. The crag was actually a nearby rocky outcrop masquerading as a distant summit. It only appeared higher than the seated climbers to my altitude-fogged brain. Joy replaced despair.

We plodded slowly past the seated climbers. They seemed to be speaking German, so I said "Guter Tag. Wie geht es Ihnen? (Good day. How are you?)" They just sat there, slumped, avoiding my gaze. OK, don't respond. I know, my accent is terrible, I thought. Maybe you aren't German. Maybe you're too tired to reply. Maybe you don't speak to strange women on Everest. No hard feelings. I'm unstoppable now, I chattered happily to myself.

As we passed the seated climbers, I savored every moment. My eyes started to fill with tears of relief and joy. I willed myself not to cry. Not now, keep your wits about you, I instructed myself. We got to a small area where wind had swept away all snow and ice, exposing gray limestone. This must be the place where Victor had told us we could find summit rocks. "Summit rocks! Gotta get summit rocks!" I mumbled through my oxygen mask. "Summit first!" growled Tendi impatiently. "OK," I replied agreeably, "Don't let me forget summit rocks on the way down." Back in Base Camp I had promised Mark, the Barts' media guy, summit rocks in exchange for some of his hand warmers.

Tendi and Nima were a few steps ahead of me. I could see nothing higher than them. They turned to face me, grinning, as I stepped up onto the snowy summit mound. I threw back my head, filled my lungs, and belted out my signature summit howl with all my might, "AAAHHHOOOO!!!!!" The Sherpas flinched in surprise. Then they grinned and howled back. I exploded into giddy laughter, delighted by their imitation. I felt as though I could leap effortlessly to the moon. After all the challenges – political, physical, and interpersonal – I was standing on the highest point on earth, against the odds. I really did it! I'm standing on top of Everest! I'm in heaven!

I started to shake Tendi's hand then impulsively pulled him and Nima into a clumsy three-way hug. We laughed and collapsed into a lean-to of Teletubbies in our oversized down parkas and pants. Chortling, Tendi and I pounded each other's chests to clear away bibs of ice from the frozen moisture of our breath. "We did it, guys! Thank you, thank you!" I said over and over. Unlike the documentaries I had seen, Tendi, Nima, and I had the summit to ourselves. "What an unexpected gift! Thank you, Chomolungma!" I murmured.

Tendi led me to the very highest point, a bench of snow flanked by a few spent oxygen cylinders and strings of prayer flags. "Sit here, Carol Didi. Don't lean back, or you fall into Tibet," he ordered, a hint of dry humor leaking past his oxygen mask. Obediently I sat. I could not resist looking over my right shoulder behind me. Tendi was right. It was a very long way down, thousands of feet down. My head swam. I carefully turned my head to look straight ahead again and sat leaning forward a little, away from the terrifying drop behind me.

Time stood still. Each precious second seemed like a life time. We could have been on the summit 10 minutes or 30 years. I could not say. I was lost in timeless wonder. From where I sat, a vast magical panorama stretched before me. The rest of the Himalayas, including the world's other highest peaks, except for K2, seemed much lower than where I sat. They looked like ethereal white islands floating in a sea of fluffy clouds, a place where angels might drift peacefully below us, singing and playing their harps. The view had an otherworldly beauty that documentaries and photos do not fully capture. I felt so fortunate, the luckiest of women, to see this magnificent view, to have climbed this magnificent summit. I felt truly on top of the world. It was the happiest day of my life!

Carol Masheter sitting on Everest's summit, just before 7 am local time, May 24, 2008, photo by Tendi Sherpa.

Tendi and Nima giggled and chatted in Sherpa, as they hustled around excitedly, stringing Buddhist prayer flags. They took turns taking pictures of each other with me, as I helped to hold up flags and pictures of their favorite rimpoches for the camera. I asked Tendi to take pictures of me using my digital camera. He took two of me alone and one of me and Nima. Then my camera froze and refused to work. I was disappointed not to get any pictures of the view. What if my camera did not capture my summit photos? I worried. I focused on making mental images of the view of a lifetime, just in case.

As I enjoyed the view, I noticed the edges of the surrounding peaks looked a little fuzzy and yellowish, as though I were wearing amber-tinted goggles. I tried to remove my goggles and realized I was not wearing any. I blinked hard, but the yellow tint and fuzzy edges were still there. I had experienced this lower on the mountain, when we moved to a higher elevation above Base Camp. Each time my eyes had returned to normal by the next morning. Today was no worse. Of course my eyes would be a bit beat up from our windy night climb and the blasts of ice crystals, I reassured myself. I found my glacier goggles and put them on. They made my vision worse. I took them off and put them away. My excitement about being on top of the world overpowered concern about my eyes.

Self care, I reminded myself. I took off my heavy gloves, gouged open a packet of GU, and squeezed half of it into my mouth. It was stiff, sticky, and disgusting. I washed it down with the rest of the water in my thermos. I glanced at my watch and thermometer. It was just before 7:00 am, May 24, 2008, minus 15 degrees Fahrenheit, and downright balmy after our cold dark night climb.

Tendi said it was time to leave. I felt no sorrow or reluctance. I had had my summit moment. I would never forget it. Now was time to start down. The hardest part of the climb was still ahead. Little did I know how hard it would be.

No Magic Helicopter

With Nima in the lead and Tendi behind me, we began our descent.
When we climbed down to the limestone outcrop, I remembered to
collect a few summit rocks. As I tried to bend down and pick up
some, I felt like an elephant seal, fat and awkward in my bulky down
parka and pants. I clumsily scooped up some gray limestone gravel,
using my bulky gloved hands like flippers. I had taken my gloves off
for a brief period on the summit to eat and drink; now my hands
were too cold to take off my gloves and pick out the prettier pieces.
Tendi was impatient to get going and grumbled behind his mask.
Nima giggled and held my parka's outer pocket open, while I shoved
in a handful of summit gravel.

Climbing down was easier on my heart and lungs than climbing
up, but the risk of falling was greater. Human legs do not seem to
be designed for going down as well as for climbing up. Also, after
climbing through the night, my body was tired, and my brain felt
sluggish. Now my ragged breathing was not from exertion but from
fear of falling. Stronger more skilled climbers than I have died while
climbing down from the summit.

At the top of the Hillary Step, fear threatened to overwhelm me,
as I peered down the steep wall. Climbing down with only a safety
was scarier for me than climbing up. If I fell, the safety should

stop my fall at the next piece of protection. However, it would not prevent me from getting seriously hurt. If I got hurt and could not climb down on my own, I would die. I did not want to even think about getting injured up here.

You know what to do, I coached myself. Just do it. I swallowed hard, steadied my breathing, and clipped my safety onto the fixed line. I backed down the Hillary Step like climbing down a ladder – except there was no ladder. I found hand holds near my waist, made sure my safety leash was not caught on anything, and lowered myself onto footholds I found by groping with my boots. This time I avoided getting tangled in the web of old fixed lines. I slid down the last few feet and landed with a clumsy stagger in the narrow saddle at the base of the Hillary Step. Done! Relief! shouted my inner optimist.

On the jagged Knife Edge I stumbled and tripped with increasing frequency over old fixed lines, rock, and ice. The adrenalin from reaching the summit was gone, leaving only a heavy sense of fatigue. When I dropped my safety while passing a piece of protection, I had trouble finding it, even though it was attached to my climbing harness by a short leash. "Can't find your safety? growled Tendi. He took it, ran it between my legs, and clipped it onto the fixed line behind me. Every time I fell, the safety's leash cut into my crotch painfully. I fell and slipped off the same slick angled rock I had slid off during our climb to the summit. My clumsiness frustrated me. Tendi was annoyed with me, too. That was disappointing but understandable. After climbing for over 13 hours, we all were very tired and wanted to get back to Camp 4.

Tendi and Nima moved down the mountain faster than I could. Each time one of them pulled or jerked the fixed line, I lost my balance. Sometimes I fell. I told them that when they jerked the fixed line, I fell over. They did not seem to understand. I tried telling them again and again. No change. I soldiered on, stumbling and falling. Getting back on my feet each time took a lot of energy.

Suddenly my feet were dangling in empty space. What the --? My brain lurched, trying to understand what had just happened. "Carol Didi, you fall in crevasse!" Tendi scolded. "Huh," I grunted, "I didn't see it." Strange, I wondered wearily, as I supported myself with locked arms, flailing my legs to find footholds inside the crevasse. How could I not see a crevasse right in front of me? I scrambled out of the crevasse and back onto the route.

Near the South Summit I noticed that I could see my feet better through the bottoms of my eyes. Tilting my head at awkward angles worked for awhile. Then even my donut of vision shrank to nothing. Looking down past my right cheek, my red and black boots with yellow crampon straps looked like a work of abstract art, crazy zigzags of color. That was the last thing I saw.

I was completely blind. My "vision" looked like a brilliantly white featureless sheet of paper. I kept trying to see around its edges, but there were no edges. I was terrified. How was I going to get down this mountain without being able to see?

Tendi and Nima tried to make me go faster than I could grope my way down. I repeatedly told them I could not see. I asked them to radio Mike and tell him that I was blind. For some reason, they did not radio Mike. I fell every few steps, tripping over obstacles or getting tangled in old fixed lines that I could not see. With each fall, rocks and ice gouged my knees, elbows, or back. My bulky layers of clothing, pack, mask, and oxygen hoses made getting back up exhausting. Steeply angled loose snow and rock slid out from under me, as I tried to get my feet under me, balance my pack, lurch forward, and stand up.

After every fall I wanted to just lie there. I was so tired. I had not eaten or drunk anything in hours. After one fall, I dug out a water bottle from my parka's inner pocket, forced open the frozen lid, and sipped the last slushy water, which made my head hurt. My body felt like it is digesting itself from the inside. I knew I should eat something, but the very thought made my gut twist like demented snakes. Pain jabbed my knees and lower back like broken glass with each step. I wanted to be rescued from this hell.

I imagined a magic helicopter would appear in the sky and lift the three of us out of this terrible nightmare. Then a voice of reason whispered, no magic helicopter will come. We are too high on the mountain. A rescue party of climbers then, my fantasy mind pleaded desperately. The voice of reason reminded me that most climbers at this attitude have barely enough energy to help themselves, let alone someone else. No one else knows you are in trouble. I asked Tendi again to radio Mike, to let him know I could not see. Tendi did not respond. The voice of reason murmured, what can Mike do anyway? See for you? Climb back up and carry you down the mountain? Not even Mike is that strong after a long summit day. I remembered what Russell Brice and other experienced climbers have said about high altitude rescues. Twenty strong climbers might move an immobile person only a few hundred feet in a day at altitudes above 26,000 feet.

There would be no magic helicopter, no rescue party. The only way I would get down this mountain would be under my own power. Get up, I commanded myself, after yet another fall. Sluggishly I felt around for something solid for my feet, lurched forward, straightened my screaming knees, and felt ahead with one boot, then the other for another solid step. Sometimes when I was lucky I took several steps before falling. Other times I fell with each step. I fought the urge to give up, to just lie there. I got up, took a step, fell, ow!, got up, took a step, fell, ouch!, over and over again.

I thought about Erik Weihenmayer, the first blind climber to summit Everest. If he could do it, so can I. It is humanly possible, I coached myself, suppressing the knowledge that he was younger, stronger, and more skilled at climbing than I.

I was a terrible blind climber. I did not have any of the heightened senses and skills some blind people develop. Eric's achievement would inspire me for awhile. Then the magic helicopter fantasy would return, followed by the voice of reason, another step, another fall, another step.

Another dark thought began to grow. What if I am permanently blind? As much as I admired Erik, I could not imagine myself living the rest of my life as a blind person. I would rather die, I whimpered. Stop that! I ordered myself. Focus on what you need to do now. Get up. Take another step.

Suddenly I felt myself falling through space, head first. I landed hard on my right shoulder. Pain flashed through my shoulder like a bolt of lightning. The top of my humerus felt like it had popped out of my shoulder joint and jutted out past my pack shoulder strap. I yelped, gritted my teeth, and pushed myself up in an awkward one-arm push-up, something I had never done before. I felt the humerus grate back into place, searing my shoulder joint like red-hot lava. Now my right hand, arm, and shoulder hurt like the devil and were useless. Great, first I go blind. Now I can't use my right hand or arm. How can this get worse? I felt trapped in a very dark comedy. Stop whining, I ordered myself. I took a step, tried not to fall, fought for it, and fell again. I got up and took another step.

Suddenly, I was falling again, head first. I screamed, "Falling, falling!" I was tumbling down, crashing into rocky outcroppings, groping wildly for something to grab. The mountain slope sped past, snatching itself from my clumsy gloved hands. "Stop falling," I whispered to myself irrationally. I stopped. I was hanging upside down by my feet, my back to the mountain, feeling battered but in one piece. Tendi and Nima were yelling at me from above, "Climb! Go!"

I was scared and angry. Biting back my temper, I replied, "I'm hanging upside down like a bat. I can't see anything. Give me a minute to figure this out." I twisted around to face the mountain, reached up for my feet with my good arm and fumbled with whatever was snarled around them, probably old fixed lines. It took a long time to free my feet and stand up. Then I went back to the endless cycle, get up, try not to fall, take a step, ouch! Down again! Get up, take a step, keep going. Don't rest. Rest won't get you down the mountain.

Between falls I tried different techniques. On the rockier steep sections, I faced the mountain and went backwards like climbing down a ladder. Tendi shouted at me to keep my back toward the up slope, but when I did that, I fell nearly every step. Climbing down backwards was slow, but I fell less often and could get up more easily, when I did fall. Both Sherpas shouted at me each time I fell. Much of the time I could not make out what they were saying. They jerked the fixed line, as though I were an uncooperative yak. My anger threatened to boil over. I reminded myself that my falls probably scared and annoyed them almost as much as they scared and annoyed me.

On the snowier sections, I turned my back to the mountain and used my ice axe as a cane. I was stiff and sore from all the falls. Crouching low to plant the axe made my quads burn. Sometimes I stumbled into the Sherpa who was climbing in front of me. He would put my hand on his shoulder and guide me. Other times, I held hands with the Sherpa behind me. When we were lucky, we could do this for a few steps, before the terrain became too rugged for us to remain in contact. On steep ice, nothing worked very well, so I muddled through as best as I could, trying not to gouge myself or anyone else with my crampons or axe.

When we came to longer stretches of hard snow, Tendi suggested that I sit down and slide on my butt. My friends and I do this for fun in soft spring snow back home in the Wasatch Mountains. Now I was so tired of painful falls and exhausting struggles to get back up, I wanted to just sit and slide down the mountain to Camp 4. However, the voice of reason cautioned that trying to butt slide without being able to see drop offs, rocks, and crevasses was not smart. I said to Tendi, "No, not safe." I got up for what felt like the millionth time, took a step, fell, and got up again. I felt trapped in a weird mountaineer's hell of endless falling and getting up. I had no sense of making any progress down the mountain.

Again I asked Tendi to call Mike and let him know that I could not see anything. Mike must be worried, because I'm taking so long.

To add insult to injury, gut acid now spurted from my backside at unpredictable moments. My rectum felt raw and burned like the devil. Gross. What did I do to deserve this? I wailed to myself.

Occasionally I heard other climbers. I apologized, when I bumped into them, mumbling that I had vision issues. I was so thirsty my tongue felt glued to the roof of my mouth. I could not remember ever being this thirsty before. Perhaps I would climb faster, if I had something to drink, I reasoned. The next time I fell, I took off my pack and groped inside for my insulated one liter bottle. The water was frozen, as Mike had warned. My stomach reacted by squeezing itself like a sponge, as though trying to force its last moisture into my blood stream. OK, so there's no water. Sitting here moaning about it won't help, the voice of reason said. I got up, took another step, fell again, got up, and took another step.

A Lifetime Ago

After what seemed like hours of falling and getting up, I heard other Sherpas greeting us. Was I dreaming? Hallucinating? We could not be near Camp 4, because we were still climbing down. Camp 4 was in a vast more or less level saddle. Tendi told me to sit down. Someone changed my oxygen cylinder. As I breathed in the oxygen, warmth and energy tingled pleasantly through my body. Apparently I had been without supplemental oxygen for some time. Groping blindly for an offered cup of what smelled like Sherpa tea, I spilled most of it. The few warm sips I was able to drink tasted like elixir from the gods. Some of our climbing Sherpas must have climbed back up from Camp 4 to meet Tendi, Nima, and me.

After our refreshment stop, we got back onto our feet. As we moved slowly down the mountain, I could hear foot steps on either side of me as well as in front and behind. We must have been a strange little procession, graceful young Sherpas surrounding a stumbling blind American woman in her 60s.

Eventually the terrain felt less steep, then more or less level. Do I dare hope that we were in the South Col? I felt my knees start to buckle. The voice of reason said, if we are in the South Col it's a big place. We are not in Camp 4 yet. Buck up. I stiffened my knees and groped with my feet, trying not to stumble over rocks and ice.

Finally I tripped through what felt like the old ripped tents, broken tent poles, and other garbage I had seen before we began our summit climb. That was only yesterday, but it felt like a life time ago.

I could hear the hiss of stoves and new voices. Gentle hands led me to a tent. Someone helped me shed my pack and crampons. I clutched their hands and murmured my thanks. I had been climbing for 19 hours, during which I had drunk less than one liter of water and eaten a tablespoon of GU. We all had had a very long hard day.

I crawled into the tent like a tranquilized salamander. Robyn's and Ang Dorje's voices greeted me cheerfully. They graciously offered to help me take off my boots. "No, no, I can do this," I thanked them and groped at my feet. They insisted on helping me. I was embarrassed but grateful. They wanted to take off my down pants too. "You don't want to go there," I said with a sheepish grin. "Thanks anyway. I'll do it later."

The afternoon drifted by like a pleasant dream. For some reason, Ang Dorje, Robyn, and I did not talk about the climb. Perhaps it was too new, too sacred to discuss, but it felt like a silent bond among us. We all were Everest summiters now. Sherpas brought us soup, then noodles, then hot drinks. Robyn and Ang Dorje took turns placing warm mugs into my gloved hands. I got better at not spilling their contents. I felt wonderful – tired but radiantly happy.

I suddenly began to cry. Robyn asked, "Are you OK?" "I'm fine," I croaked, "These are summit tears, happy tears. Such a gift, such a gift!" I sobbed, probably making no sense. I was embarrassed. Then I remembered an Ecuadorian guide, Javier Herrera, saying to me as I wept on the summit of Cotopaxi four years ago, "Real mountaineers weep, when they reach the summit." Robyn and Ang Dorje graciously gave me emotional space, until my tears had run their course.

Before sunset, I was able to distinguish Robyn from Ang Dorje. She was a light shape. He was a dark shape. It was not a very difficult distinction, but my vision seemed to be returning. Again I wept with joy. I just hoped I could see well enough to get down the Lhotse Face tomorrow without being a liability to anyone.

After sunset Robyn and Ang Dorje drifted off to sleep. I got busy removing my down pants, my Saturn suit, and diaper. I cleaned myself and my clothes with frozen travel wipes as best as I could. It was a slow clumsy process, but the mess was not as bad as I had expected. I changed out of my summit socks and into the now dry socks I had worn the previous day. After one more swig of water with my evening meds, I settled into my sleeping bag.

I was very tired but still too excited about reaching the summit to feel sleepy. Images from the past 24 hours kept replaying inside my head, the vast sparkling Milky Way, the diamond pendent of other climbers' headlamps snaking up to the Balcony, silent lightning illuminating cumulus clouds below us, the last steps to the summit, howling with the Sherpas, our three-way hug, my timid glance down thousands of feet into Tibet, the sea of clouds and its mountain-islands at our feet, prayer flags, rimpoche pictures, summit photos. I will remember these beautiful images for the rest of my life.

After today's ordeal, my body and mind desperately needed rest. I tried to relax and fall asleep. My legs had other ideas. On their own, they started marching in clumsy shuffling steps inside my sleeping bag, like a dog running in its sleep. I commanded my legs to stop. They did -- for awhile. Then they started marching again. I told them to stop again. The crazy marching went on and off throughout the night. I wanted to laugh and groan with frustration at the same time. I had never experienced anything like this.

At times my oxygen mask felt like it was suffocating me. I made myself wear it at a flow rate of one liter per minute. I needed to recover from today's climb to be strong for tomorrow's descent. In the wee hours of the night, I noticed the oxygen flow had stopped. I sat up and tried to get the oxygen flowing again without waking Robyn and Ang Dorje. The regulator showed the tank was not empty, but still no oxygen flowed. The line must have frozen. Finally I gave up.

I was more comfortable anyway without the claustrophobic mask and its Darth Vader noises.

May 25. By morning, my eyes were goopy and sore, and the slightest breeze made them burn, but my vision was nearly normal. Again I wept with gratitude and relief. We took our time getting ready for our descent down the Lhotse Face to Camp 2, drinking tea, eating breakfast, and packing. Ang Dorje had noticed a tear in my down pants and had stopped the hemorrhage of down with duct tape, which I appreciated. I wore my ski goggles to protect my sensitive eyes. It was time to start down.

Getting my big boots and crampons down the Geneva Spur was more awkward than climbing up, but it went well. I was not as tired as I had expected to be after yesterday's challenges. Perhaps I became overconfident. While descending the Yellow Band, I took a nasty spinning fall and mashed my lower back on the rocks. No serious damage resulted, but the deep bruising made me even more lame and sore. I learned later my fall caused Tendi behind me to fall. He was not hurt, but the fall broke the oxygen collection bottle between his cylinder of compressed oxygen and mask. Tendi was OK, but I felt bad about making him fall and the damaged gear. I offered to pay for repairs.

As we passed other groups, our guides proudly told their guides, "Seven out of seven to the top." I felt a bright happy glow each time I heard the pride in their voices. Our summiters included seven team members plus four guides and twelve climbing Sherpas, 100% of those who started from the South Col. That was great by any standard.

We blew past Camp 3 onto the steeper sections of the Lhotse Face. My previous descent of that long exposed icy slope had terrified me. I had descended in a tense quad-burning crouch. I did not look forward to doing that again. Snow had fallen since we were last here. It had bounded well to the steep ice and made the descent of the Lhotse Face easier than expected. I blazed down it and arrived in Camp 2 just behind Robyn, our fastest team member.

Camp 2 was my least favorite Everest camp, yet it felt great to be here. Jangbu's meals, which had been so unappealing a few days ago, tasted good now.

I Felt the Earth Move Under My Feet

After a night's rest, we left Camp 2 and headed down to Base Camp through the Khumbu Icefall for the last time. I had mixed emotions. The Icefall was stunningly beautiful with its wonderfully weird shapes and shades of turquoise, but it was scary and dangerous. More seracs had shifted or fallen, and new crevasses had opened. Fallen ice debris had buried more of our fixed lines since the last time we had climbed through the Icefall. The Ladder Bridge From Hell, my biggest hoop of fire, now sloped downward so steeply I could down climb it backwards, like climbing a ladder down from a roof. It was easy, a welcome surprise.

As the climbing season came to a close, the icefall doctors were less conscientious about maintaining the route. In the Popcorn Tendi picked up a ladder bridge, which had come completely unanchored, and moved it to another part of the crevasse. Crossing this unattached ladder was unnerving, but it held. During my climb of Kilimanjaro 6 months ago, our guide, Ben Marshall, had told me about his terrifying fall and rescue after a collapse in the Khumbu Icefall. Later I learned one of the ladder bridges slipped, while Nikki was crossing it. She avoided a fall, but she was understandably shaken. The Icefall was full of surprises, some not pleasant.

After the Popcorn section of the Icefall, Tendi and I stopped for a brief rest to drink, snack, and shed layers of clothing. Suddenly a loud crash exploded to our right. We both flinched then crouched like hunted beasts. "Shit!" I squeaked. "Sheet…" Tendi echoed. A huge avalanche was spilling down the edge of the Icefall, thundering ominously. The glacier shook under my feet. "I feel the earth mo-oove under my feet," sang Carole King crazily inside my head. We watched the avalanche's terrible beauty, as huge cauliflower clouds of spindrift billowed up and swept over us. "Tendi Bai, I think the mountain is asking us to leave," I murmured weakly. "Yes, Carol Didi, let's go," Tendi agreed. We exchanged wan smiles and continued the convoluted route down through the Icefall.

The adrenalin rush from the avalanche drained my body of the rest of its energy. The demands of the summit climb had finally caught up with me. I felt like a rag doll. My knees hurt like the devil and did not work very well. I hobbled through the ice maze like a geriatric goat. My injured shoulder and back were killing me. My eyes stung. Mucus glued my eyelashes together. I tried to focus, but I stumbled frequently, especially during the steeper down climbs through jumbles of ice blocks. Don't blow it now, I reminded myself. It would be really stupid to get hurt, so close to the end of the climb. Tendi sometimes disappeared ahead, impatient with my slowness. No doubt he was tired too and wanted to get to Base Camp as soon as possible. I flashed back to my own impatience with climbers who were slower than me on Kilimanjaro and on hikes back home. Now I was the one who was annoyingly slow. Karma, I thought wryly.

The hours dragged on. It was hot. At a small safe zone, I stopped and stripped off more layers. This felt like the slowest of my trips through the Icefall. At times I did not want it to end. This was the last real climbing on Everest. Other times I wanted it to be over. It will take as long as it takes, I told myself.

In Lower Lake Land, many of the frozen lakes were now open water. Some of the narrowest of these new lakes now had ladder bridges. Yuck! More ladders, my inner whiner grumbled. Better to cross ladders than swim through ice water, my inner optimist replied. The larger lakes we had to go around, making the route longer. It was weary work.

After an eternity or two, Simon and Laurel met us near the toe of the glacier. Simon insisted on taking my pack. I gratefully let him. We went a little further together to find a place to sit. Simon and Laurel had brought soda pop and snacks. I wanted a Coke. None were left, so I settled for a Sprite. Tendi had a beer and sat a little apart from us. He was quiet and remote, perhaps tired and glad the climb was over. I pulled out the zip lock bag of Gummi Bears Laurel had given me before I left Base Camp and showed them to her. I told her that when I felt discouraged, I pulled out that little bag and read what she had written, "Summit Gummi's for Carol, you can do it! ☺". I wanted Laurel to know how much her gift meant to me.

After our rest, I stumbled toward Base Camp, taking what seemed like a very long time. I even started to stumble down off the route, until Tendi shouted at me. At last, I saw the familiar boulders and prayer flags that marked our home for the past six weeks. I howled, "AAAAHHHOOOO!!!" Several howls floated back. I laughed, crazy with joy. One last awkward scramble up talus, and I was in camp. Warm hugs and welcomes from guides, other climbers, and Sherpas greeted me. Chhongba had outdone himself with a fabulous lunch of sushi, cheese, and dried blueberries and cherries. Everything tasted heavenly, especially the blueberries and cherries, the best I had ever eaten.

After lunch, I requested warm water for a shower. In the shower tent, I looked at my face for the first time in nearly two weeks in a little mirror. A red-eyed creature with spiky gray hair and zebra stripes of sunburn stared back. I laughed at my wild woman reflection, until my sides hurt. I stripped and looked down. My ribs jutted out like an old-fashioned washboard. I ran my left hand down my lower back and felt more protruding bones. Several impressive bruises from my many falls were in full bloom. After my nightmarish blind descent, I was grateful all I had was bruises and a very sore right shoulder.

Taking a shower at 17,600 feet elevation was a bracing experience. The warm drizzle from a suspended bladder of warm water quickly evaporated from my skin and hair, snatching warmth from my body. Brisk scrubbing with soap stripped off layers of sunburn, dried skin, and climber stink, as I balanced on tender feet and stiff knees. I chafed warmth back into my shivering body with my swimmer's towel and pulled on clean clothes. They were a lot roomier than when we arrived at Base Camp six weeks ago. I felt wonderful -- lean, clean, and very pleased with myself.

May 29. The next few days slipped easily into pleasant rest day activities. We ate leisurely breakfasts of made-to-order omelets while sitting in the sun. I washed clothes, read, relaxed, and packed my personal gear in preparation for leaving Base Camp. Tears of joy and relief about our summit and safe return overwhelmed me at unexpected moments. Our climbing Sherpas made trips back through the Icefall to dismantle our camps higher on the mountain. We cheered and applauded every time they returned. They still grinned shyly. I was relieved to have made my last trip through the Icefall, but it was not over, until all Sherpas had made their last trip and returned safely.

People from other expeditions stopped by our camp. A group of young researchers asked for saliva samples to look for genetic markers for effective acclimatization to high altitudes. "Sure, sounds interesting" I answered. I spit into a vial, until I was dry.

A young woman stopped by Lydia's sleeping tent next door, while I was organizing my stuff. She and her boyfriend had been members of another expedition. Her boyfriend had became seriously ill and had to leave, while she stayed. She said that the other expedition members, all men she had not known before this trip, were not supportive, and she did not summit. Her voice broke with emotion, as she added she had a medical condition and had had abdominal surgery for it. Her hand swept up her shirt tail to reveal an impressive looking surgical scar. "Maybe I'll try to have a baby. For me that would be harder than climbing Everest," she said tearfully.

Lydia suggested that if she tried Everest again, an expedition company with deep resources like Adventure Consultants would give her a better chance for the summit. "Carol here crapped out on the Lhotse Face, and she summited," Lydia added. I bristled. I did not "crap out." During my first attempt up the Face, I made a decision not to climb it, when I felt unwell, to avoid putting others at unnecessary risk.

That said, I agreed with Lydia. Our expedition had supportive guides and deep resources. We had plenty of food, fuel, oxygen, and other supplies. They had been willing to take a chance on me. A guide with another expedition had given up his chance for the summit, so his clients would have more oxygen cylinders and therefore a better chance at summiting. This guide's personal sacrifice was generous and professional. However, his client climbers then had one less (or no) guide to the summit. An expedition with deep resources would not require such a sacrifice of the guide.

I could understand this young woman's distress and disappointment. I probably would have been as upset, if I had not summited. However she worried me. She seemed so sad and defeated, looking for some other difficult challenge, perhaps to prove she was a worthwhile person. A bit like me, I thought ruefully.

Not summiting was not the only emotional challenge. One of my team mates seemed remote and down, though he had summited. Perhaps he was experiencing a let down, not uncommon after finishing a big undertaking. I did not feel a let down yet, but I probably would in a few weeks. Already, I was asking myself, now what? What does an amateur woman mountaineer in her 60s do after summiting Everest? Is the best part of my life over? Will it be a downward spiral of shrinking abilities from now on?

The Dance of the Wounded Bear

After dinner, the Sherpas joined us in the mess tent, looking shy and awkward. Something seemed to be in the works, but nothing much was happening. I almost left to rest in my sleeping tent. Then Laurel cranked up the iPod, and bottles of rakshi, the local distilled spirits, appeared and were passed around. Some of us moved tables and stacked chairs to make dance space. Shoulders relaxed a little, but we still stood around like shy teenagers. My dance phobia, left over from my awkward adolescence, kicked in, but I did not want to miss anything. Robyn sang an aria and then taught us a simple cancan. Arms around each other's shoulders in a big circle, some guides, team members, and younger Sherpas imitated her moves. The Sherpas were very attentive and copied her meticulously.

The iPod shifted to a lively dance tune. Lydia broke the ice and started dancing solo. She was all lithe arms and legs, writhing like an enchanted wild woman. Robyn joined in, then Cheryl and Nikki and some of the younger Sherpas, all making stylish moves. Simon danced as though he were possessed, perhaps exorcising demons from a failed Base Camp romance. Lhakpa, one of the few older Sherpas who was dancing, out-styled everybody.

I caught Mike's eye. He looked as awkward as I felt. Then I noticed Victor, Phil, and Steve were missing. I was strangely comforted to know that I was not the only one who felt awkward. Mike started dancing cautiously near the edge of the scrum of dancers. His courage inspired me. What the hell. I jumped in and started flapping and flailing, riffing on some of the other dancers' moves. At best I danced like a wounded bear.

Dancing at 17,600 feet elevation was a surreal experience. When I got too dizzy from the thin air, I stopped to rest and sip a Coke. No sooner than my bony Everest-wasted butt found a plastic chair, young Sherpas rushed over, grabbed my hands and pulled me to my feet, "Dance, Carol Didi, dance!" How could I refuse? At one point, they even invited me to solo in the center of the circle. I silently shouted down my inner critic and danced for all I am worth, leaping, whirling, possessed by pure joy. I had so much to celebrate: our summit, the return of my eyesight, our safe return to Base Camp, everyone's hard work that had made all this possible. Joy rushed through my body in great soaring waves. Dancing like a maniac, I alternated between tears and laughter. I would not have missed this dance for a million dollars.

"Sherpa song, Sherpa dance," we team members chanted. The mood shifted. Slowly all the Sherpas, even those who had not been dancing before, stood. We put our arms around each others' shoulders in a circle. The Sherpas sang, timidly at first, then more boldly. They taught us some simple steps, not unlike Robyn's cancan. Once the Sherpas started this dance, it went on and on, as though it had a life of its own. We swayed, stepped, and sang, united by our Everest experience.

Finally, at around 10 pm, I left the mess tent reluctantly. Though I did not want to miss a single moment of this once-in-a-lifetime celebration, my body hurt from all the falls, and I needed to rest. Mike and Ang Tsering ended the party not long afterwards, so the climbing Sherpas could get some sleep. They would get up early to make one last trip through the Icefall tomorrow to finish clearing our higher camps. As quiet spread through Base Camp, I settled contentedly in my sleeping tent. I did it! We did it! We stood on top of the world! This happy chant inside my head sang me to sleep.

The next morning, some team members were planning to fly by helicopter from Pheriche to Lukla. Steve was organizing the flight. He was talking to members of other expeditions to share the cost of a full helicopter. Steve was in his element, having a great time wheelin' and dealin'. It was great to see him having so much fun.

I was torn. I had always wanted to fly in a helicopter – as long as it were not a rescue helicopter hauling my sorry self out of a situation I should have been smart enough to avoid. Also I did not look forward to hiking 45 miles in three days, especially with my injured shoulder, bruised back, and sore knees. However the helicopter flight cost as much as my round trip air fare from Salt Lake to Kathmandu. Besides, I wanted to spend more time with my team mates, savoring our climb and camaraderie. I vacillated for a couple of days, while we were preparing to leave Base Camp. Steve was very gracious and patient with my indecisiveness. Lydia said flights in smaller helicopters were more fun than the larger ones that fly from Pheriche. That settled it. I told Steve I would walk to Lukla instead of fly. My first helicopter flight would have to wait.

May 28. It was time to say goodbye to Base Camp. The familiar cluster of tents had been home for six weeks. I was sad to leave this haven of comfort and rest on the world's highest mountain, the scene of so many emotional ups and downs. Herds of yaks arrived to carry down loads of gear and trash. Other expeditions were packing and preparing to leave too. I went looking for Mike Hamill, with whom I had climbed Aconcagua, but he had already left. Part of a big climb is coming full circle, returning home and seeing friends, telling tales and hearing about what had happened in others' lives while I had been away. As sad as I was to leave Everest, I looked forward to going home.

Life After Everest

After three days of long flights and long waits in airports, I arrived at the Salt Lake City International Airport. I was tired from the climb, days of travel, and too little sleep, but I felt peaceful about being home. As I walked down the stairs to baggage claim, I noticed a group of about two dozen people at the foot of the stairs. They were cheering and waving signs, balloons, and pompoms. They must be welcoming home a Mormon missionary, I smiled to myself. Then I heard someone say, "Is that her? Is that Carol?" I glanced down at myself. My cleanest climbing pants hung from my scrawny hips like gang-banger pants. With my unruly hair, sunburned zebra-stripped face, and baggy clothes, I was not sure I would have recognized myself.

I looked again at the welcoming party and saw the Executive Director of the Utah Department of Health, Dr. David Sundwall. He and others were wearing home-made paper hats with photos of Everest and me on them. I recognized more friends from the Wasatch Mountain Club, my meditation sangha, my workplace, and even my former workplace. They cheered and waved; a few were even dancing. Friends hugged and congratulated me. The fatigue from the climb and the long flights vanished. I fumbled to find words to thank them.

A guy with a microphone and a vaguely familiar smile approached me. I recognized Brent Hunsaker, a local television news reporter, with a camera man in tow. I sat on the floor and downloaded pictures from my digital camera to the camera man's laptop, while some of my friends found my duffel bags in baggage claim. Then Brent interviewed me about my climb with the camera rolling. "At an age when most people are thinking about retirement," he said, "You climbed the highest mountain in the world. What's next?" I still had not fully processed my Everest experience and had no plans, other than settling back into my usual life of bicycling to work and playing with friends in the nearby mountains.

After the interview, about a dozen friends took me to dinner at the Red Iguana, a popular Mexican food restaurant. As we passed through several dining rooms, Vickie McDaniels, one of my Wasatch Mountain Club friends, announced, "This woman just climbed Everest!" Roomfuls of complete strangers beamed and applauded. I did not know what to do, except smile shyly, and murmur "thank you" over and over again. I had not imagined such a welcome home in my wildest dreams.

Later that evening, the airport interview with Brent Hunsaker was broadcast with pictures of my climb appearing and dissolving in the background. A local daytime television show invited me to appear in a live broadcast, right after a family of clog dancers and a self-styled mountain man wearing buckskins. Several local newspaper reporters interviewed me and ran stories about the woman in her 60s who summited Everest. Complete strangers recognized me in the grocery store and congratulated me. Some asked for autographs and wanted pictures taken of me with themselves and their children.

Dozens of people followed the dispatches on the Adventure Consultants web site and my emails during the ten weeks I was away. Some people stayed up all night during the summit climb and followed the online progress report. Jan Orton even sent email to Adventure Consultants asking to hear more about me.

The Wasatch Mountain Club gave me a welcome home dinner at our lodge in the mountains and presented me with a bronze plaque commemorating my climb. My pictures were not ready, so I did an impromptu question and answer session. People were rapt. Between their questions and my answers, I could have heard a pin drop in the packed lodge.

After my pictures were ready, I was invited to give numerous other talks. I have spoken at the local Recreation Equipment Inc., the Winter Festival at Bryce Canyon National Park, two lock-down drug rehabilitation centers, a local prison, an exercise and physiology class at the University of Utah, an alternative high school, a class of fourth graders, an assembly of sixth graders, a group of older lifelong learners, various hiking clubs, and several private gatherings. I met people I would not have met otherwise. Again and again, the interest and enthusiasm of so many diverse groups of people in my climb deeply moved me. Since I was a little girl with polio, I secretly wanted to be just a little bit famous. Now that I was a little bit famous, I did not know quite what to do. I was like a dog that chased cars and finally caught one.

The day I stood on the summit of Everest, I was 61 years and 7 ½ months of age. As of this writing, I am the oldest American woman and the second oldest woman in the world to have summited Everest and survived the climb. Recently, several experts have said that people in their 60s should not climb Everest. In the summer of 2010, Chinese officials started restricting climbing permits for the route through Tibet to applicants 18 through 60 years of age. Around the same time, Nepalese officials announced restrictions for the route through the South Col to applicants 16 years of age and older.

I too have concerns about the abilities of very young and very old climbers on Everest, as well as those who lack appropriate experience, skills, and fitness. Because so few people under age 20 and over age 60 years have been on Everest, findings based on their small numbers are not very reliable. That said, the death rate for Everest climbers in their 30's and 40's is higher than for climbers in their 50's, 60's, and 70's. In my opinion, each climber deserves to be considered in terms of his or her mountaineering experience, skills, and fitness rather than age alone.

I would like to continue climbing as long as I still enjoy it and do not endanger others. However, two problems remained. The temporary blindness I experienced during my descent of Everest needed to be addressed, before I attempted more big mountains. Back at home in Salt Lake City, my eye specialist, Spencer Mortensen, and a high altitude vision specialist and mountaineer, Geoff Tabin, could find nothing wrong with my eyes. Dr. Tabin thought the extreme altitude might have triggered a severe migraine aura-like disturbance to my vision. Other medical professionals have suggested very low blood sugar or localized pressure on the optic nerve or retina might have temporarily blinded me. My vision returned within 12 hours, whereas snow blindness, retinal bleeds, and corneal lacerations need more time to heal. We know more about what did not cause the blindness than what actually caused it. I would like to try another 8,000 meter peak, but it would be unwise given my history with temporary blindness on Everest.

Another problem was the extreme shortness of breath I experienced above 20,000 feet elevation. I consulted Colin Grissom, a mountaineer and pulmonologist with expertise in high-altitude respiratory problems. He ordered tests. Though my VO2 maximum (a measure of the maximum amount of oxygen a person's tissues can absorb and utilize) was nearly 60 ml/k/min., which is off-the-charts good for men and women of any age, my pulmonary function was only about 75% of the average for women of my age, including those who are ill or not very fit.

Dr. Grissom said my test results suggested mild asthma. I was skeptical. I had used long-term and short-term asthma medications on Everest, but they did not improve my breathing. Dr. Grissom prescribed Advair, another asthma medication. I tried it before and during my attempt on Denali's West Buttress route in 2009. Even at home, Advair made me cough and reduced my voice to a hoarse whisper. It did not help my breathing on Denali.

In 2010, I returned to Denali and summited without any asthma medication. For the summit climb, I wore a Talus Cold Avenger face mask. Two days later, when we hauled all of our gear from Camp 3 down to the glacier plane landing strip through the night in 9 ½ hours, I did not wear the mask. I had a substantial asthma attack during the last hours of that haul. The trigger seemed to have been long hours of high exertion while breathing cold air. On any future high altitude climbs, I plan to wear a mask to keep my airways moist and warm.

Some say Everest changes you. I hope it changes me for the better. Certainly the people I met and the experiences I had during my Everest climb provided good lessons for my post-Everest life. The Namche woman who returned money I had overpaid for a yak bell exemplified a universal sense of ethics that transcends culture. The "enemy" who became an ally on the Lhotse Face reminded me to be open to positive changes in even the most difficult relationships. My blind descent to Camp 4 was a powerful lesson in staying calm in a life-threatening situation and persisting when it would have been easier to give up.

One change I have noticed is an increased urge to "give back." Many people face their own personal "Everest," whether it is fulfilling a lifelong dream or facing an unwelcome challenge like cancer, addiction, or prison time. My Everest talks are one way I can give back, particularly to people who feel discouraged or powerless. If my talks inspire just one person to live a dream, fight the good fight, or make wiser choices, perhaps I can help make the world a better place.

As I reflect on the climb, Everest continues to teach me new lessons in humility. A good part of summiting Everest is luck. The mountain does not care how fit, skilled, or experienced a climber is. I am lucky to have climbed in relatively benign weather on Everest.

My body apparently has the right genes to acclimatize to Everest's altitude and function well enough to summit and survive. Taking credit for my genes or the weather seems silly, like boasting about the color of my eyes.

That said, I believe thorough preparation improves luck. Before attempting Everest, I "paid my dues." I gained over a decade of experience in high-altitude mountaineering and learned the needed skills before attempting Everest. I learned from mistakes, both my own and those of others. I bought the best clothing and gear I could afford and climbed with one of the world's most deeply resourced and experienced mountaineering companies. I trained hard to be in peak physical condition for the climb. During the eight weeks I spent in the Khumbu, I did acclimatization climbs to trigger adaptation to high altitude balanced with sufficient rest, so my body could get stronger and not burn out. I balanced persistence with caution. Thorough preparation and these choices increased my chances of summiting and returning home safely.

I am not an expert. This is not a how-to-climb-Everest book. However, it does describe how I prepared, the climb, and what it was like for me. It was the climb of a lifetime that I will remember until the end of my days. I hope others find it interesting and useful. Whatever your dream or challenge, plan well, prepare well, and go for it! AAHHHOOOO!!!!

CPSIA information can be obtained at www.ICGtesting.com
228537LV00006B/182/P